Pursuing BAD GUYS

Joining Children's Quest for Clarity, Courage and Community

Donna King

Edited by Ann Pelo
and Margie Carter

Exchange Press

ISBN 978-0-942702-74-3
eISBN 978-0-942702-75-0

© 2021 Donna King

Book Design: Stacy Hawthorne
Production Design: Kaitlyn Nelsen
Editors: Ann Pelo and Margie Carter
Managing Editor: Tina Reeble
Production and Copy Editor: Erin Glenn

Photos provided by Donna King with special thanks to Children First parent photographers Al Sun and Melissa Eggleston. Photos on pages 115–117 © Adobe Stock.

This book may not be reproduced in whole or in part by any means without written permission of the publisher.

For more information about other Exchange Press publications and resources for directors and teachers, contact:

Exchange Press
7700 A Street
Lincoln, NE 68510
(800) 221-2864
ExchangePress.com

for Fred Rogers,
who made me feel safe and good
when I was little, and who still calls
me to my best teaching self

There's the good guy and the bad guy in all of us,
but knowing that doesn't need to overwhelm us.
Whatever we can do to help ourselves—
and anybody else—discover that's true,
can really make a difference in this life.

MR. ROGERS

A NOTE FROM THE EDITORS

A Call to Reimagine Our Work

The stories in the *Reimagining Our Work* (ROW) collection are anchored in the conviction that another world is possible for early childhood education—a world characterized by open-hearted and attentive collaborations between children and educators, in shared exploration of engaging ideas. This collection helps us begin to imagine that world, as we reimagine our work, moving beyond the joyless land of prescribed curricula with its corresponding outcomes and assessments, into the unpredictable, green-growing terrain of lively curiosity and rigorous critical thought.

Too often in our field, the discourse about educators reflects a diminished and disrespectful view of their capabilities for challenging, rigorous, generative thought. "Keep things simple and easily digestible," is a common caution. "Teachers want strategies that they can put immediately to use in their classrooms. Don't offer too much theory, too much complexity."

We disagree. **Strongly.** We believe that educators hunger for deeper meaning in their work. We believe that educators long to be challenged into their biggest, deepest, most startling thinking and questioning. We believe that educators are ready to have their hearts cracked open and their imaginations ignited. We believe that educators are eager to explore how theory looks in everyday practice and how practice can inform theory. These convictions are at the heart of this collection of stories.

In these stories, children and educators take up ideas of substance, pursuing questions in ways that are unscripted and original. They braid fluid imagination and expansive awareness into their collaborative inquiry. The children in these stories aren't "gifted" or privileged—except by the gift and privilege of their educators' potent regard for their capability, and their concomitant willingness to bring their best minds and hearts to the table.

Which is just what we see the educators do in these stories.

We hear educators reflect—in their unique voices and contexts—on their evolving understandings of children's capacities, and their roles as educators, and the meaning and practice of teaching and learning. The educators in these stories hold assumptions and visions different from the dominant paradigm in our field, and we have much to learn from them.

With the ROW collection, we hope to advance the conversation among early childhood educators, administrators, community college and university educators, policy makers and funders about the nature and practice of early education—a conversation which we also engage in the foundational book for this collection, *From Teaching to Thinking: A Pedagogy for Reimagining Our Work*. As you read, we hope that you are challenged, exhilarated, unsettled, and rejuvenated. We hope that you find kinship in these stories. We hope that the stories in this collection carry your thinking far beyond curriculum ideas, and help you reimagine your work. May these stories sustain you as you stand strong with the children in your care. Resist the limitations of standardized curriculum, and claim, instead, the exhilaration of creating a new world, together with children.

—**Ann Pelo** and **Margie Carter**
  Editors of the *Reimagining Our Work* (ROW) Collection
  Authors of *From Teaching to Thinking: A Pedagogy for Reimagining Our Work*

For more information on the ROW collection and upcoming titles please visit ExchangePress.com/ROW

CONTENTS

FOREWORD 11

INTRODUCTION: BEGINNING THE YEAR 17

1   LEARNING ENCOUNTERS 25
    My Own Disequilibrium...27
    A Pedagogical Companion 28
    Reciprocally-Created Research..29

2   A CULTURAL SHIFT 37
    Inviting a Conversation about Bad Guys 43
    Listening, Not Rushing...47
    The Group as Our 13th Child...48

3   BECOMING BAD GUY RESEARCHERS 51
    Research Questions and Hypotheses 52
    Generating a Bad Guy Lexicon 53
    Making Our Research Visible 56

4 ACTION TO SUPPORT OUR RESEARCH 59
- Creating a Shared Drawing 60
- Inviting the Bad Guy into Stories 62
- Watching for Bad Guys in Pretend Play 73
- A Pretending Game about Badness 76
- Making the Bad Guy Pretending Visible 82

5 OFFERING MATERIALS FOR BAD GUY RESEARCH 87
- Bad Guy Action Figures 88
- Bad Guy Self-Portraits 94

6 PROTECTION FROM BADNESS 103
- Pretend Play about Protection 104
- Stories about Protection from Badness 108
- The Teacher's Role in Protection 111
- A Provocation about Protectors 113
- A Parent Survey about Protectors 124

7 FINDING POWER IN SHARED STORY MAKING 131
- Fumbling to Find a Way Forward 132
- Not a Globe, but a Book 135
- From Clarity to Confusion 146
- A Roller Coaster of a Conversation 148
- Momentum, Flow, and Finishing 163
- The Good Guys Take the Day 175

CONTENTS

8   GOODBYE TO THE FADING BAD GUY 179
    Crafting Rituals around Goodbyes 180
    The Funeral..183

9   REFLECTING ON LEARNING AND CHANGE 191

ACKNOWLEDGEMENTS..199

ABOUT THE AUTHOR 201

STUDY GUIDE 203

FOREWORD

Good guys versus bad guys. Children are tapped into this archetypal dynamic that has threaded itself into story across centuries and cultures. Odysseus and Cyclops, Duncan and Lady MacBeth, Red Riding Hood and the Wolf, Robin Hood and the Sherriff of Nottingham. Dorothy and the Wicked Witch of the West. Black Panther and Killmonger. Harry Potter and Voldemort, Luke Skywalker and Darth Vader. Hero and villain. Good and evil.

Archetypes point us towards spiritual and psychological truths about being human. They ask us to confront essential questions about the meaning of our lives and the workings of our world. They call up philosophical ideas that shape our understandings of the human condition. The most resonant archetype that threads through myths, religious stories, and pop culture is the Hero, an ordinary person drawn into a journey in which she confronts fear and danger and disruption. During her journey, the Hero forges her character, calling on qualities that she hadn't recognized in herself in order to persevere—in order to vanquish villainy.

Children are on a quest to understand what it means to be human, and their dramatic play and stories are rich explorations of ethical human truths that are exposed in the confrontation between good guys and bad guys. "Children have an innate desire to be good people," Donna King writes in her deep-dive into *Pursuing Bad Guys*. "Becoming good requires grappling with badness."

And grappling with badness is messy, loud, fierce work. It often makes educators edgy and out-of-sorts, turning us stern and sanctimonious. We squash bad guy play with bans on improvised "weapons." We try to reduce its power to narrow lessons about perspective-taking and empathy, asking the children to consider bad guys' birthdays and moms. (At least, that's what we did when we were teachers!)

What happens if we allow the mythic narrative of good guys versus bad guys to play out in our classrooms, making room for children to step into the compelling, ancient, necessary confrontation between badness and goodness, resplendent with terror and courage and heroism and ferociousness?

That would be a bold, brave act for an educator to take, and that's what we see Donna do in *Pursuing Bad Guys*. She and her co-teacher, Sarah, commit to stay present to and curious about children's bad guy play, in all its noise and fierceness and running and yelling and tackling and battling. They recognize the potency of this play for the children's *becoming*, and understand that the children are joining a lineage of people determined to look directly at elemental goodness and badness as a way to understand the complexity of their own human souls. Donna explains: "The [children's] stories are allegory. It's Good versus Evil, and the children are Good. With our tricks and our team, they are saying—on behalf of ourselves and those weaker than ourselves, without grown-ups to help, to the point of exhaustion, without giving up—we will put a stop to this Badness."

But Donna and Sarah do more than simply make room for—and honor—children's bad guy play. They tune themselves to this play as a way to practice new ways of being teachers.

This is not a quick-and-easy decision. They had "made peace with our little school" as it always had been, Donna writes. Until suddenly and achingly that peace is unsettled by an encounter with what *could* be. During a visit to a school rich

FOREWORD

with stories of collaborations between children and teachers, Donna writes, "Almost in spite of myself, I get curious about what it's like to watch for the ways that children play out and represent ... a topic or question that has urgency and staying power." From a place of "longing, hope and fear," Donna chooses to make a deep dive into the arena of in-depth investigations co-constructed by children and teachers, and to invite a pedagogical companion to guide her journey.

Pursuing Bad Guys is a story of courage. The children embody courage as they confront villainy, pushing past fear into bold action. Donna and Sarah embody courage as they commit to grow towards their longings, unsettling the familiar and easy and comfortable. They move from "just watching" and documenting children's bad guy play—which they've always done with terrific respect for the play—to becoming active provocateurs in the children's pursuit of bad guys. And that takes trust. Trust in themselves, to "move from the sidelines and into the action ... in a way that is not intrusive, but informed" and is in service to the children's agenda. Trust in the children, to receive their teachers' provocations with curiosity and willing engagement. Trust in Pam, the pedagogical companion that Donna and Sarah have chosen, to walk alongside them with respect and with frank challenge.

This book's subtitle is important: *Joining Children's Quest for Clarity, Courage and Community*. This is a book about quests, and quests require trustworthy companions. Donna describes the layers of trust this way: "We wanted to sound to the kids like Pam sounded to us. And the kids trusted us to hold the space for their work like we trusted Pam. We all trusted in the process, trusted that the purpose would guide us. And because of all that trust, we could all learn." **That** is co-construction in practice—co-construction of thinking, yes, and co-construction of community.

Civil rights activist Valarie Kaur, the founder of the Revolutionary Love Project, asks us to "look at others and say: You are a part of me I do not yet know." This seeing is at the heart of trustworthy companionship. What courage it takes to open ourselves to each other in this way! Co-construction is vulnerable work. It requires us to turn towards our companions with an expectation that we will be changed by our work together—that we will grow more fully into ourselves. We look at our companions with curiosity: "What aspect of *that* person is waiting for me to find in ***myself***?"

When we move from this expectation of discovery, we're poised for learning—about ourselves and about our companions.

"You are part of me that I do not yet know," Donna says to the children, and settles herself in to listen and to learn. "You are part of me that I do not yet know," Donna says to Pam and to Sarah and to the children's families. And all those folks say it to each other. Donna, Sarah, Pam, the children, and the children's families trust in each other's contributions to the evolution of their thinking, their understanding, their capacity for vulnerability, their courage to act.

Donna's writing calls us to expand and strengthen our capacity for courage and community. It invites us to seek trustworthy companions, to move through self-doubt and take up our own quests, to confront our fears and embrace our longings. And it reminds us that the certain outcome of our quests is evolution, as we become ever more fully ourselves.

—Ann Pelo and Margie Carter

Editors of the *Reimagining Our Work* (ROW) Collection

Authors of *From Teaching to Thinking: A Pedagogy for Reimagining Our Work*

INTRODUCTION

BEGINNING THE YEAR

It's August 29, 2016—the first day of a new school year at Children First. My co-teacher Sarah and I are here with our "old-timers"—the eight children, mostly four-year-olds, returning from last year. Just for today, our small preschool is all theirs—a few hours to reconnect with us, with routines, with materials and with each other after a summer apart. Tomorrow, we will begin welcoming the "new-timers"—the younger children who will join the group this year.

The morning is almost gone when Miles offers to help Sarah fill the water tables, where he is quickly surrounded by a busy crowd, pumping colored water into soapy mixtures. Sarah is there, observing with camera and notebook in hand, as the mixing becomes pretending:

Elisabeth: Actually I'm making a smoothie.
Parker: I'm making Gatorade and if you eat Gatorade, then we put it in the stranger's mouth that comes into our town.

Elisabeth: Yeah, the bad strangers.
Parker: Yeah, bad strangers that come into our town.
Sarah: How do you know they're strangers?
Parker: Because we don't know them.
Sarah: But why do they need to drink the Gatorade?
Parker: Because we're nightmares. We are bats that make this kind of yucky stuff that's called Gatorade.
Elisabeth: Yeah. I make Gatorade, too.
Parker: That means you're bad.
Elisabeth: It's a poison and it…
Parker: Yeah it's a poison and it can kill people.
Elisabeth: It can kill *bad* people.
Sarah: So how do you tell the difference between someone who is a bad stranger and someone that you haven't met yet, like someone's grandma who's coming to visit?
Elisabeth: You look at their body. We just like, look at their body and you just *know* and we say-
Parker: …and we say, 'hold on!' and then we go and get the Gatorade and put it in their mouth. Then their eyes close and their arms go straight out.

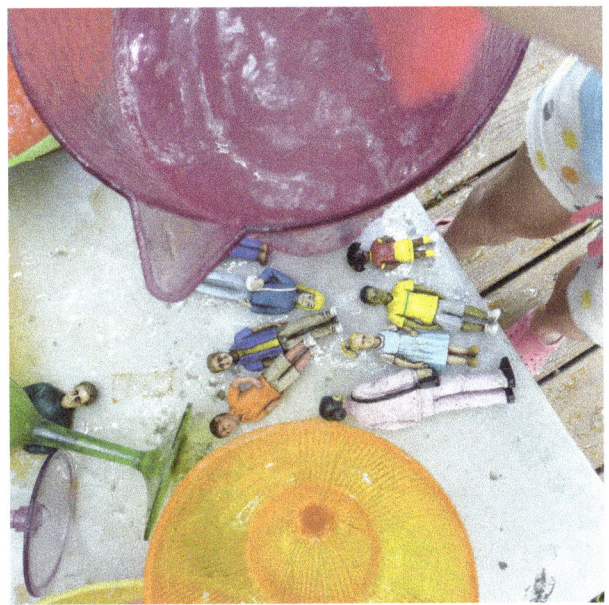

*Gray indicates educator

Avery has been listening; now he reaches into the bowl of play people figures on the shelf, chooses a little man, and steps deftly into the game.

Avery: Hey, a stranger is here!
A stranger is here!

Agreeably, the girls drip their Gatorade over Avery's stranger, then drop the toy man in the water and pronounce him dead. Now Elisabeth digs into the bowl of people figures, and finds a "whole bad family" that needs to eat Gatorade… and so it goes, until a big pile of bad strangers has been satisfactorily dispatched.

I smile when Sarah tells me about this game. Sure, the content seems dark. But the energy of the players is relaxed and light, flowing in an easy dance of dialogue and action, grounded in the children's sense of belonging in this place and with each other. And in fact, there ARE strangers on the way. Tomorrow the new-timers arrive. Having already lived in this school community for a year or more, the old-timers are well aware of their real-world obligation to welcome these actual strangers with respect, curiosity and generosity. Perhaps, I think, this game is a way of working through some trepidation about what lies ahead.

And in my view, that's the power of this kind of pretending. It's not just "permissible mischief."

> Pretending to be one way—
> in this case, defensive and
> aggressive—actually bolsters
> the children's capacity to
> act the opposite way—open
> and welcoming.

The game provides a safe way to metabolize problematic feelings and impulses. Pretending is like releasing a big deep breath; it clears tension, and frees up the emotional energy that children need to become the decent people they aspire to be. For this reason and many more, Children First teachers have always supported the children's play about serious content, including their play about badness in all its forms.

Children First families hear a lot from us about how and why we embrace pretend play that includes bad guys, violence and weapons. It's a perspective shaped by the work of Diane Levin and Nancy Carlsson-Paige, and informed by our trust in children's drive to make sense of their own tumultuous feelings and the complexity of the world around them. We believe that children have an innate desire to be good people, and we understand that becoming good requires grappling with badness. Our families read about pretend games like "Poison Gatorade for Strangers" in the portfolios they take home each week, and they hear about this kind of play in their afternoon check-ins with teachers. So they are familiar with the particular ways their own child—and their children's friends—work with this sort of content.

And now more than ever, questions of "good" and "bad" have a grip on our collective attention. We are in Durham, North Carolina, a blue city in a red state. When this school year begins, our nation is on the verge of electing Donald Trump, who has campaigned loudly about "dangerous strangers" with brown skin—Mexicans, Muslims, African Americans. Our state is embroiled in divisive arguments about transgender rights and fair elections. Some of our families are politically active; all of them are concerned. In this amped-up anxious atmosphere of high-stakes conflict, our own longstanding values as teachers—values about embracing difference and respectful debate—have been and will be relentlessly tested. When we teachers are feeling so riled up by the actions of our political "opponents"—people who stir our righteous anger and spark such fierce and censuring language—we feel a bit disingenuous in our usual response to the appearance of bad guys in story and play; it's harder to suggest, as we often have, that bad guys have Moms and birthdays and understandable reasons for their actions. It's not as easy as it used to be to stand with our hero Fred Rogers in his belief that "There isn't anyone you couldn't love once you know their story."

Meanwhile, Sarah and I—and indeed, Children First itself—are ripe for a mid-life crisis. Like many American preschool teachers, we have long defined our practice with words like progressive, child-centered, play-based and developmentally appropriate. We love Lillian Katz, Elizabeth Jones, Sydney Clemens, Vivian Paley, and Bev Bos. At the same time, we've been intrigued by stories from the alternate universe called Reggio Emilia; our 20-year study of the teaching and learning there has felt like a long tug of war between inspiration and disequilibrium. We are awestruck by the intellectual, emotional and aesthetic depth of the long-term co-constructed investigations at the heart of Reggio-inspired teaching.

But despite my liberal philosophy, I have a deeply conservative temperament. Like a child who watches and watches before joining the play, I need to feel sure before I do anything, and I would rather do nothing than do something wrong. And though Sarah is more open to risk, she and I are both compelled in very real ways by our school's history and traditions, by our individual skill-sets and comfort zones; and by our collective attachment to "how things have always been." We are what we know how to do and have done before. In this school where individual children are always and visibly changing and growing, Sarah and I wonder—can we, too, step into the current of learning, development and becoming?

CHAPTER 1

LEARNING ENCOUNTERS

A few weeks later, in October 2016, I attend a conference at The Sabot School, a well-known Reggio-inspired program in Richmond, Virginia. Sarah had visited there the year before and found it inspiring, but I'd been resisting seeing it for myself. It was easy to blame my reluctance on time and cost, but truthfully, I was worried I'd come away feeling inadequate, as I often do when I look closely at other people's exemplary programs. Still, in just a few months, our city was set to host the Wonder of Learning exhibit from Reggio Emilia, and along with the exhibit would come lots of professional development opportunities. I'd already decided that this year I would give myself the chance to be a learner who doesn't shame herself about what she still needs to learn. Going to The Sabot School was the first test of my resolve.

And who should be opening the conference but Pam Oken-Wright—a teacher whose brilliant work I had been following for so long that I'd even given her a private nickname: "The Venerable Oken-Wright." In her talk, Pam is charged with introducing us to "the qualities of a Reggio-inspired program." She walks us through a chart, and in my mind, its components become a checklist for considering what happens—and does not happen—at Children First.

There are a few things I think we do well...
- Image of the Child as competent, resourceful, driven to create relationship and find meaning.
- Environment as the Third Teacher—ordered, beautiful, readable, alive.
- Emphasis on Relationship and Collaboration.
- 100 Languages—for making thinking visible and speaking from the heart.
- Documentation—creating traces of the children's process and thinking.

And there are a few things I think we do to some extent...
- Emphasis on Construction of Theory. Discourse, debate, listening.
- Teacher as Researcher. Reflecting and making our own learning visible.

And then there's that one thing we don't do at all:
- Reciprocally-created, in-depth investigations.

The co-constructed investigations that many consider the very heart of Reggio-inspired practice—what we've heard described as "tossing the ball" back and forth between teachers and children—never seem to "work" when we try them. Either we have no idea what to offer, or we offer something that doesn't really interest the kids, something less alive and important than what they would be doing if we'd simply left them to play. After a few attempts here and there over the years, we've pretty much decided that this part of Reggio-inspired teaching is not for us. We do a lot of things well, we tell ourselves, and what we do is enough. We've made peace with our little school as it is.

But almost in spite of myself, I get curious as I listen to Pam describe what it's like to watch for the ways that children play out and represent a repeated intention—a topic or a question that has urgency and staying power. I flash back to my years as an English major, sensing that, in the practice Pam is describing,

teachers study the children's work the way a literary critic studies a novel, looking for meaning in themes and imagery, and, especially, searching out the motivations and developmental arcs of the characters.

That's something I understand, and love to do. And really, it's not that different than the way we currently observe and write about children for their individual portfolios.

Pam explains what comes next. Once the teacher has identified the children's intention, she asks herself, "How can I support that intention with the questions I ask and the materials I provide?" And then the teacher offers something—just a little something—and watches "what happens" with open-minded curiosity. Now Pam has turned from thinking, which I like, to action, which I find mystifying and scary. It's that "offer a little something" that has seemed like an awfully big unknowable something when we've tried this way of working before.

My Own Disequilibrium

And then Pam describes the unhurried and spacious nature of this process, as the teacher allows time for each unfolding moment in the ongoing conversation between provocation and response. Unhurried? Spacious? My heart constricts. Our days with kids feel packed with action, offerings, invitations, competing opportunities and NEVER enough time. We come to the end of the day like a base runner sliding into home plate. When Pam uses these words, I feel the pull of a familiar and painful inner conflict between my desire to MAKE as many good things happen as much of the time as humanly possible, and my longing for a gentler pace and an expanded sense of time. Could it be possible that this other way of working—which I have long imagined as *more* rigorous—might actually lead to school days that feel less relentlessly effortful?

And if that perplexing possibility wasn't enough, Pam brings another lightning-bolt word into the conversation: "trust." She says we must "trust that there will be richness in the process itself as the children go as far as they are willing in their investigation." I believe that I do trust children, but I see now that trusting the children is not enough; I have to trust the process, and trust myself and my co-teacher IN the process. I don't have that trust, and suddenly I'm quite sad about that. And I'm sadder still when Pam concludes with the words: "The by-product of this demanding way of teaching is joy."

In my sadness and confusion, I realize that maybe I'm not quite as content with "good enough Children First" as I thought I was. And then I think: "I'm 55 years old. If I don't try this now, then when? Am I really willing to give up the possibility of teaching this way without trying one more time?"

In this state of mental and emotional disequilibrium, I spend a few hours experiencing The Sabot School: speaking with their thoughtful teachers, observing the brilliant atelierista in her studio, and reading documentation of the beautiful work these adults have co-constructed with children. And now I find myself almost underwater, swimming in a sea of longing, hope and fear. When she is this close to drowning, even a conservative person will make a decisive move toward an unknown shore.

And so I move.

A Pedagogical Companion

I approach Pam with a specific request. Would she be willing to work with Children First? By that I mean, would she be willing to get to know us as we are now, and then, from that place of understanding, tell us what we will need to change if we are going to attempt that unchecked item on her chart: Reciprocally-Created In-Depth Investigations? Her answer is "Absolutely." And we are on our way.

We arrange an intensive two-day visit with Pam, one day for her to learn Children First, and another day for us to work together on next steps. From there, we'll continue the conversation via email, until Pam returns for a second visit. We work out the financials with our Board and set a date. Our work together will begin in January.

On the Thursday before Donald Trump is inaugurated, Pam comes to Durham. She has already read our website, our weekly newsletters, and reams of portfolio entries. Today, she watches us move through our daily routine, and observes the children interacting with one another, with materials and with us. She chats with kids and parents, occasionally asking questions as the day unfolds. And at the end of the day, once the children are gone, she sits down with me and Sarah to debrief.

As Pam prepares to share her observations, we feel the piercing vulnerability of opening ourselves to evaluation from someone whose opinion we respect so deeply. The question of whether she will "get" us feels scary enough. More worrisome is the possibility that she *will* see us clearly and discover some mortifying inconsistency between what we profess to be and what we really are, revealing fractures in our fundamental integrity.

So it's a sweet relief when Pam makes it clear how much she appreciates the relationships, routines and environment we have created. Listening to her warm and detailed observations, Sarah and I feel seen and safe. In the way of all caring teachers, Pam is walking us onto the solid ground of self-confidence that learners need to feel beneath their feet before they can step into the unknown.

This is a significant moment, one that we will re-experience many times with varying particulars over the coming months. Sarah and I, with our different learning styles, will need and ask for different things from Pam along the way. But for both of us, the foundation of our relationship with this pedagogical companion must be what I call "reciprocal confidence." We already know that Pam is a brilliant pedagogue, but now that she has demonstrated clear-sighted respect for us, she is OUR brilliant pedagogue. We are fully confident in her, which gives her the power to loan confidence to us.

> And that's what good teachers do for their students: loan them the confidence they need to move in the direction they long to go.

That crack in the sidewalk looks like an abyss until someone you trust takes your hand, and you realize that with just a baby step or two, you can jump right over.

Reciprocally-Created Research

And so we step, as Pam dives straight into the heart of our big question: What would we have to do differently, here and now with our children, to enter the arena of in-depth investigation—what she calls "reciprocally-created research?"

Her answer: "Much less than you think... We are talking about a small shift in perspective and priorities." And, she continues persuasively, "I am convinced that making that shift will yield rich results."

And then she offers us a way in, a concrete first step. She shares a little snippet of conversation she recorded that morning in an area of our play yard where we've created a Sand River. She came across three boys—Sam, Miles and Avery—building a dam to create a "mushy puddle" for killing bad guys, and arguing about whether God is a real person.

In the midst of that conversation, the dam broke, and the boys cheered.

Pam:	Is that what you wanted to happen?	Miles:	Carving wood.
Sam:	Yeah! That was the whole idea!		
Avery:	Yeah, remember, they [the bad guys] come down the slide, and then the boat goes in there, and then they jump in the mushy and the mushy makes them die, right?	Whoops and hollers from the boys.	
		Pam:	Where are the bad guys now?
		All:	WE'RE the bad guys!
Pam:	Is it the mushy that makes them die? (Yes) What is the mushy made out of?	Pam:	Oh, YOU'RE the bad guys! So you're going to bury yourselves?
		All:	No. No.
		Sam:	We bury the good guys.

LEARNING ENCOUNTERS

Sarah and I are not surprised by this incident—we've been watching play like this all year, beginning with that poison Gatorade at the water deck. We've just never considered DOING anything about it. In our minds, this sort of play is important, but it belongs to the kids. We enjoy watching it, and we sometimes document it as a way of tracking the children's concerns and relationships; but we would not get involved unless the players need support with a conflict or reminders about safety. We would not want to intrude, or insert our agenda into the children's play. We're the teachers who joke, "Don't just DO something! Stand there!"

But Pam is pointing us to a different sort of involvement in the children's play. She wants us to listen to the children more deeply; to study their play as a window into their thinking, emotion, and, especially, their intention. As our pedagogical companion, Pam wants us to listen with the intent to act. This has been where we've tripped up in our earlier attempts at in-depth investigation. We are reluctant to take action, because we don't want to derail the children's play. And, even when we're willing to act, we're unsure about what action to take. It's been more comfortable for us simply to listen and document. Pam is asking us to change how we see our role.

We will listen, yes, but not simply to document.

We will listen in order to connect with the children's thinking and emotion, and to align with their intention, in a way that is not intrusive, but informed, and therefore genuinely respectful and responsive.

In this way of working, teacher action does not interrupt, but, instead, meets up with the children's agenda. Even more compelling, Pam is convinced that the teacher's involvement—when sensitive enough—can help children move from mere preoccupation with a concern to a sense of mastery and empowerment around that concern. We are unsettled but intrigued.

Pam says, "Now you have to decide. Are you willing to risk moving from passive observation of the children's bad guy play to active listening? Away from the sidelines of the play and into the action?"

In fact, Sarah and I have already made that decision. Pam has won our trust. When she says "I think this is a good idea," we would feel like we are cheating ourselves if we don't at least give that idea a try.

And if we are going to try building an investigation with the kids, studying "Bad Guys" has particular appeal. We know that these kids—like most preschoolers we've known—are already preoccupied with thoughts and feelings about good guys and bad guys. We don't worry that inviting further consideration of this intrinsically interesting topic will force children to expend energy on something they don't care much about. We're glad, for example, that Pam is not suggesting we study "dams" or "rivers"—topics that were also present in the conversation she'd recorded. There's nothing remotely dry and academic—or as Sarah would say, nothing "school-y"—about the juicy topic of "Bad Guys." And the topic resonates for us personally as well. After all, we are living in the same super-charged and divisive cultural and political context as the children.

So we are ready to say "Yes" to joining the children in an investigation of badness. But we still don't know what that "yes" entails, exactly. What do we *do*, right now, with this enticing bit of bad guy talk? We literally have no idea.

Pam suggests that we take "a snippet of conversation, something you observed, some shared moment or an observation" back to a group of children. For example, she says, "There are some potentially powerful comments in this conversation. You can invite the boys to tell you about being bad guys trying to bury good guys. Or you might say to all of the kids, 'Do you ever pretend to be the bad guys?' Or 'What do you think about bad guys burying good guys?' Or even 'What do you know about good guys and bad guys?'"

She goes on to say, "Realize that you may not get any engagement with the question you ask. The conversation may go to another place altogether. That's OK and good. Also realize that this is new to the children, so it may or may not take time for them to figure out that you are really asking for their opinions."

So, okay. One next step is a conversation, a reasonable option for these verbal children, who share fluency in a common language and already enjoy the give and take of lively dialogue. Anything else?

Pam urges us to think about the role that representation might play in this investigation. She reminds us that working in many different languages—

like drawing, and movement, and sculpture—is vital to the learning process, because we all have to represent an idea in some way in order to understand it. And representational languages offer unique perspectives and complexities, different than spoken languages. We talk with Pam about our children's familiarity with using representational languages. Certainly, they draw quite a bit. They illustrate their stories; make mail for each other and for their families; "sign" their work by drawing their personal symbols; and draw as part of their play (including, this year, countless treasure maps). And Sarah regularly invites children to draw from life, often as part of "looking closely" at plants and animals. But we haven't regularly asked children to represent their thinking in drawing. That will be new territory for us to explore together.

Pam encourages us to step into this new terrain with courage and curiosity, acknowledging that we will make mistakes and feel clumsy and uncertain. "Give yourself space to be on a learning curve here," she says. "Try to relax and enjoy it."

So, as Pam heads back to Richmond, Sarah and I have our assignment. We will continue to LISTEN—to document and then reflect on the children's bad guy play. And we will take action, inviting the kids to share their thoughts and feelings about bad guys in two ways: talking and drawing. We'll do the talking and drawing with kids in groups, instead of working with kids one on one in our usual way. Sarah and I agree to divide the work: Sarah will try some drawing, and I'll see what happens with talking. These seem like do-able—even enjoyable!—ways to step into that current of shared becoming that we will soon be calling Bad Guy Research.

CHAPTER 2

A CULTURAL SHIFT

With Sarah, the kids have been working with photographs of their faces as part of an ongoing conversation about skin, hair, and eye color. Today, she asks them to consider those familiar photographs in a way that may connect to their thinking and feeling about "Badness." She places sheets of transparency paper over the faces and invites children to come to the table in pairs. There, she offers color sharpies and says "Change your face to make it scary."

All the children are happy to give it a try, and the results are interesting.

Take Elisabeth & Alena, old-timers who typically choose friendly and nurturing roles in their play; the closest they get to Bad Guys are transgressive kitties and naughty babies. This invitation takes them into some new territory...

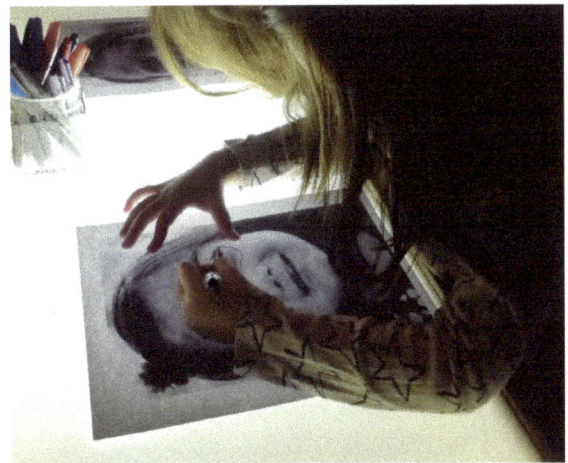

Sarah: Talk about how you changed your faces. What was your idea about that?

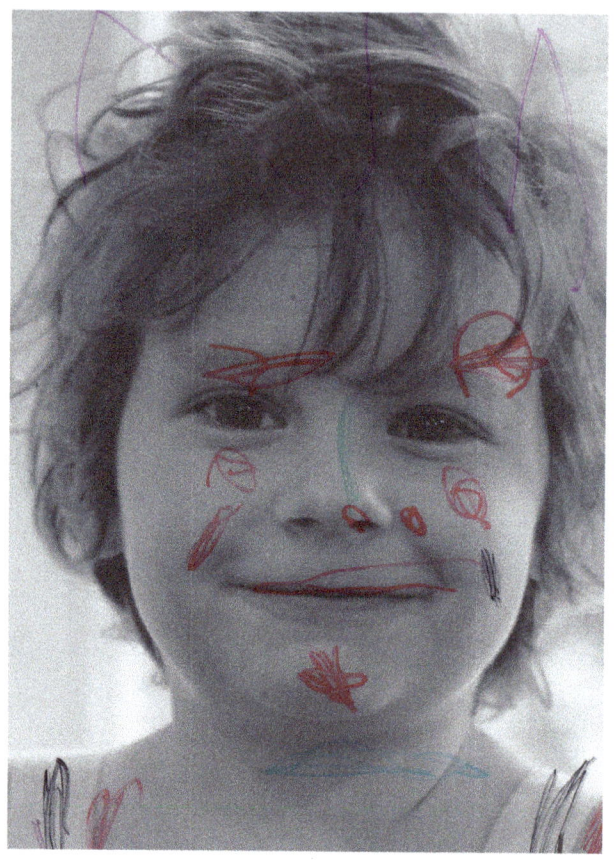 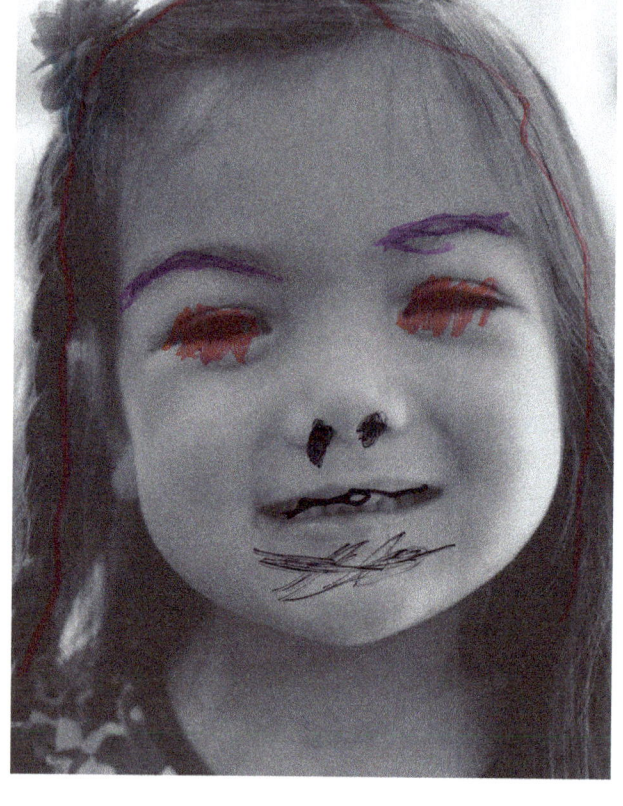

Alena:	Just like a zombie or something?		Elisabeth:	I'm a zombie, too, and my mouth is weird.
Elisabeth:	And I made mine with scribbles around my chin. I made a crown, too.		Elisabeth:	A zombie like, "Ooooh, zombie." They're scary.
Alena:	And I made different hair.		Sarah:	So you made yourself look scary?
Sarah:	What's a zombie?		Elisabeth:	Yeah. The crown is just decoration.
Alena:	A scary thing. And I did it by changing eyes, I guess.		Sarah:	Are zombies good guys or bad guys?

Alena: Bad guys!
Elisabeth: Yeah, that's why on my crown the pointy parts have bombs shoot out.
Sarah: I wonder why you didn't draw over your eyes, Elisabeth.
Elisabeth: I just like my usual eyes.

Elisabeth makes it clear—there are limits to how far she is willing to go into the badness, and her eyes are not to be involved.

And here are Sam and Parker, both 5. You met Sam—easy-going, resolute and insightful—in our play yard's Sand River with Pam. And it was Parker who began her year with Poison Gatorade for Strangers. Parker is a strong presence—most days, I would say, the Alpha presence— fiercely opinionated and sometimes quite anxious, driven by her high energy and uncompromising intellect. When Parker and Sam collaborate, they usually find common ground in humor: two serious children who somehow help each other lighten up.

Parker: I put green seaweed on my eyeballs.
Sam: I put a robot mouth on me with freckly hair.
Parker: I put glasses on.
Sam: And scary ears.

A CULTURAL SHIFT

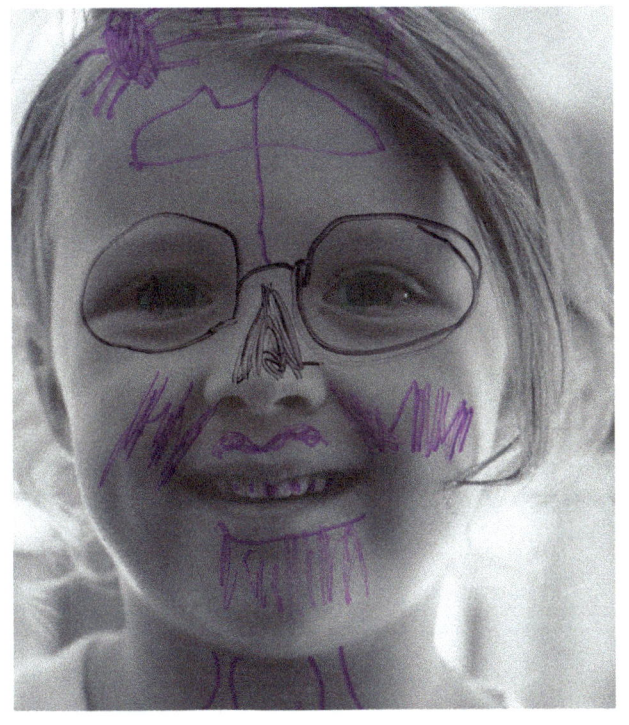

Parker: And I had a spider in my hair and I had a mustache and a beard.

Sam: And my tooths were dirty.

Parker: And I have scary purple teeth!

Sarah: I heard you both use the word 'scary.'

Sam: Yeah. Cause I like being scary and scare people in real life.

Sarah: Are scary things good guys or bad guys?

Both: Bad guys.

Sam: I like to be scared a lot of times. I like doing the scaring.

Parker: I like doing the scaring.

Sam: Actually I like doing both.

Parker: I like doing both. I would never get scared.

You can feel in this playful dialogue a dynamic that will characterize much of the Bad Guy work to come—the dance between hilarity and horror, and between genuine bravery and false bravado.

Inviting a Conversation about Bad Guys

Meanwhile, I invite Parker and Elisabeth to join Sam, Miles and Avery, the boys in the original conversation with Pam, at the outdoor picnic table, right beside the Sand River where the original conversation unfolded.

This sort of gathering is a novelty; we have rarely, if ever, convened a group for conversation in the middle of the morning. Our group conversation typically happens at lunchtime when we are already sitting together in a relaxed way, because I've always been skeptical about whether it's age-appropriate to ask preschoolers to sit in a group just to listen and talk. Pam does not share this skepticism, and she's got me curious about what a group conversation might feel like early in the day when the kids are fresh.

I come to this gathering with a firm intention. I will hold the space for conversation, and my attitude will make it clear that I believe talking together is both important and fun, worth our time and worthy of our attention. It's true that I'm completely unsure of myself, but I've watched Pam work now, and I think I can at least approximate her confident, relaxed and alert way of holding herself in a group conversation. I will keep Pam's suggested questions in mind, but I don't want to be attached to any particular outcome for the conversation. My aspiration for this meeting is to allow myself time to think about what I want to say or ask next, without getting distracted or frustrated by digressions or silly energy. I want to be gentle and generous with myself, and with the children, as we step onto this new terrain.

We talk for about 15 minutes. I am pleasantly surprised by how willing the kids are to leave their play and engage, and pleased with the overall energy of the gathering, which feels like an authentic, kid-friendly mix of serious and silly.

Donna: Here's why we're here. When Pam was here, she was hanging out by the Sand River, and there was a game she thought was really interesting. And I thought it was interesting, too. Sam, Miles and Avery, will you tell Parker and Elisabeth a little about the game where you were the bad guys, and you were burying good guys?

Sam: And it didn't work. Because... it just never came over the slide that we meant it to.

Donna: It never worked to actually bury the good guys?
Sam: Only some.
Avery: The boats float down the big slide and then the boats crash into the hole and the good guys jump out of the boat and they jump out into the water and then they die and then we bury them. And then after they read about them on the stone, we break the stone.

Listening later, I realize I'd conflated two things the children had been talking about in these conversations: the idea of killing the good guys and the idea of burying them. I'd been assuming that burying was the method of killing and now I began to see they were thinking about an actual burial, like a funeral.

Donna: What do y'all think about bad guys burying good guys?
Avery: GREAT.
Miles: Great. Since bad guys are just like that, yeah, bad guys have guns. And they break the stones with what their life was like—
Donna: Oh, you mean the stone that marks where they're buried?
Avery: Yeah.
Donna: They break their gravestones?
Many: Yeah.
Donna: Why?
Avery: Since we're mean.

There's a pause, and I take a breath. Normally, I would stop when the kids stop, cut them loose to play, and turn this little discussion into a simple portfolio entry. But this time, I decide to carry on, offering a question that occurs to me as potentially useful for learning more about the children's thinking around the difference between bad guys and "regular people."

Donna: I have another question for you about gravestones. If a bad guy dies, what happens to him?
Avery: They just bury him and then we break the gravestones.
Donna: Does a bad guy have a gravestone?
Avery: They just put him in a tree and then they die.
Parker: Bad guys are not real.
Donna: Oh I'd like to hear more about that Parker. What does real mean?
Miles: Like you're real.
Avery: You're real.
Elisabeth: I'm real.

Sam: I'm real.

Parker: I'm real, they're just imaginary things.

After a few conversational twists and turns...

Avery: I'm ALWAYS a bad guy. Since I like being bad guys.

Donna: You have a grin on your face when you say that. (A little pause). If bad guys aren't real, how do you know how to BE a bad guy?

Miles: Since I AM a bad guy.

Parker: Because you can pretend whatever you want a bad guy to do.

Avery: You can kill the bad guy.

Donna: A bad guy can kill a bad guy?
Avery: No, a nice person can kill a bad guy.

I notice that Avery is quite fierce on this point. We'll hear more from him in the future about the importance of nice guys protecting people from bad guys.

Donna: Do bad guys ever fight with each other?
Many: No!
Donna: Are bad guys on the same team with other bad guys, and they don't ever kill each other?

I'm alert to any mention about teams, because we have seen an intellectual and emotional pre-occupation with that word all year. "Teams" are everywhere: at the lunch table, on the basketball court, in the block area. Teams are building dams, raising pretend families, hiking at the river. As all these teams form, re-form, and define themselves in various ways, the sub-text remains the same: "Do I belong?" Now I wonder: will teams be part of any potential bad guy endeavor?

Many: Uh huh.

Sam: Actually, sometimes they fight. Over who is gonna fight the good guys.
Parker: And they hide in tall grass. And they are really good climbers and jumpers and they can climb trees and jump off of them and land really safely.
Donna: So you're saying they have some powers to do things.
Parker: Well, not powers, but they can do a lot of things. Like they can jump over bushes and leap from a tree and land safely everywhere.
Donna: Bad guys are grown-ups?
Parker: Uh huh. And if you were playing a bad guy game, it's a grown-up game.
Sam: You know what's kind of cool in Star Wars? That one of the bad guys that was a storm trooper turned into a good guy?
Donna: That can happen? A bad guy can turn into a good guy?
Sam: Actually he wanted to be a good guy.
Donna: That's super interesting to me, Sam.

And a little more wandering around, until...

Donna: OK, let me ask you one more question, and then I'll cut you loose to play. We've done all this talking about good guys and bad guys and now I'm curious about what you'll play today. So here's something you said earlier and I'm wondering about it. You said that bad guys are grown-ups and if you're playing bad guys it's a grown-up game. What were bad guys like when they were kids?

Parker: They were not bad guys. They learned to be bad guys. And they had pretend shooters and then they got real shooters.

Sam: Or maybe they had shooters that shoot strawberries.

Donna: OK, we're going to stop now. But I want you to go away with a question in your mind. And the question in your mind that I will ask later—is "How did it happen that the good little kid with a friendly shooter turned into a bad guy?"

Listening, Not Rushing

Sarah and I enjoyed this work with the children. We did not feel like we were forcing anything; we could feel the children's energy and interest feeding our own curiosity and excitement. It really did have that sense of spaciousness and natural momentum that Pam had spoken about at The Sabot School.

And, after just these two "tosses of the ball," Sarah and I have so many conceptual questions we want to pursue with the children: Are bad guys real or pretend? If kids are never bad guys, how do bad guys end up getting bad? Do bad guys like being bad? Can they change? Is badness always scary? And, and, and...

We send the transcription of our conversations with the children and copies of their drawings to Pam, and the three of us discuss it over e-mail. Pam acknowledges the engaged energy of all involved. But about all these questions we want to ask, she is firm. By all means, make note of all the "good ideas" we have—those ideas may be useful later. But for now, slow down. Wait. Listen more. These are good questions, but they are *your* questions. What are the children's questions? She adds, "It may be too soon to assume we know what's going on. I think more image-searching (trying to uncover the children's image of badness) may be in order."

Pam's role is critical here. Sarah and I are simply feeling happy that our little forays into collaborative research went as well as they did. Pam knows enough to see that the kids can do—and, indeed, need to do—much more. She points out that the children's conversation was hobbled by the lack of consensus over the term "bad guy," and that our role might be to help them come to agreement and clarity in order to communicate and work together more effectively. Pam reminds us to be patient; to stay curious; and to take what comes as data and not as a verdict.

We need a pedagogical guide/companion for this longer view. For Sarah and me, there is a big black box between an initial idea from the kids and some kind of meaningful work created by the kids. We've heard and read so much about this process, but we can't quite make out the nitty gritty details that come between where it starts and where it ends; we can't see far enough into that black box to make a path through. But Pam has lived and worked and thrived inside that box for years and years; she knows many ways through, and can shine a light to help us see our options. With her beside us, we can trust that there are no dead-ends, just twists and turns and choices.

The Group as Our 13th Child

But before we take any path through the black box, Pam insists we need to consider a significant cultural shift.

At Children First, we do not see ourselves so much as one group, but as a collection of unique and valuable individuals—on the wall in our office, there is a hand-made poster that says "Not 12 Children, but one Parker, one Miles, one Lia, one Elisabeth, one Sam, one Alena, one Finn, one Maya, one Mical, one Avery, one Oliver and one Aiden." At this school, the well-being and development of the individual is our primary focus, and each individual's sense of belonging and whole-hearted participation in the community is our primary goal. That's why, for instance, each child chooses a sign—a visual symbol—that becomes a key part of their identity as a member of the Children First community, one which will be theirs forever; no sign is ever used twice. It's why our documentation practice focuses on telling each child's story through extensive individual portfolios. And it is also why we feel so strongly about allowing each child as much choice as possible in how they spend their time at school.

Pam understands that the individual child sits at the center of our mission, our imaginations, and our hearts. But she is saying, "Look, each of those individual kids needs to be part of a group with a coherent identity, a shared vocabulary, and a collective purpose." Listening, I have an "aha" moment:

> "Pam, maybe you're telling us that we need to think of the Group as our 13th Child, one that deserves the same attention and respect that we give the other 12."

She says, "Exactly."

And over time, as the Bad Guy Research unfolds, we see that Pam is right. The Group develops through collaboration and communication, and collaboration and communication require shared language; so, the deeper and more precise the shared understanding of terms, the better the shared work. The more we speak of ourselves as a *Group* of Bad Guy Researchers, and the more we work on developing a shared vocabulary about Bad Guys, the stronger the Group becomes—and ultimately, then, the Group has more to offer each of the 12 children who make it up.

What a powerful and grounding piece of guidance this was—a "call to action" that would shape much of what we did with children over the next few weeks.

CHAPTER 3

BECOMING BAD GUY RESEARCHERS

In a certain sense, Sarah and I had always considered ourselves research-minded teachers. After all, we constantly puzzle over individual children's motivations, emotions and challenges; make theories about how best to support each child; test those theories with action; and observe and document the results. But we have never really felt like researchers partnering WITH children to study the world around us. So, given our dislike for using powerful words in an inauthentic way, and our genuine dread of making false claims about our curriculum, we have steered clear of trendy Reggio terms like "research" and "investigation." But now, the words fit. We're excited to claim these terms for ourselves, and even more exited to offer them to the kids as a way to describe what we are doing together.

As we begin to speak consistently about ourselves and the children as "Bad Guy Researchers," our collective intentions and actions come into a sharper focus and closer alignment. We find that the words confer a kind of legitimacy on us and on our work, and that energizes us, which in turn energizes the whole enterprise.

Research Questions and Hypotheses

As the work progresses, Sarah and I draft some Teacher Research Questions—questions that capture what's interesting to us about the children's play, and that we can, as Pam says, "keep in reserve" as we continue to listen.

What are the kids trying to figure out about bad guys?

How does this play serve the children?

> *Their sense of safety? Are we safe from bad guys? How can we be safe from bad guys?*

> *Their ethical agency and identity? Am I good? Is there badness inside me? Can both these things be true at the same time?*

> *Their fun? What do we make of the evident delight the children take in this kind of play and storytelling? Especially their delight in thoroughly and unambiguously destroying and banishing badness?*

How does this work relate to the kids' preoccupation with Teams?

In the past, questions like these lived in the backs of our minds, but we never felt any real need to answer them. If asked, we might articulate these sorts of thoughts as a way of explaining our general belief that bad guy play is a legitimate and interesting way for kids to spend their time. And they were definitely the type of questions that might come up in an enjoyable one-off conversation with children here and there, conversations that felt rich and lively but that did not result in any kind of sustained group inquiry. Now, though, these questions have our full attention, and provide a context for our observations of the children's bad guy play.

And the questions spark some hypotheses, statements that help us clarify our thinking and wondering about the play. These hypotheses ground us, help us stay connected to why we are pursuing this Bad Guy research, and steady us in moments of doubt and uncertainty.

We think the children are researching the differences and boundaries between:

- *Good and bad;*
- *Making mischief and doing harm;*
- *Real and pretend;*
- *Winning and losing;*
- *Excitement / suspense / being scared.*

Meanwhile, Pam reminds us to keep our eye on the big picture with questions like these:

What is changing for the children as a result of engaging with this subject matter? What are they learning about themselves and about the world? How are they evolving?

Specifically, how will being Bad Guy Researchers help children feel a greater sense of control? Can it give them "a pocketful of positive resources" to use in the face of fear or powerlessness or challenge? Will they leave this work "feeling bigger?"

I'm beginning to understand the way in which this work happens on multiple levels at once.

We pay attention to the children's passion and curiosity in order to offer provocations that engage that energy. And we seek to understand the roots of that passion and curiosity so that we can align ourselves with those deep intentions.

Why research bad guys? Because bad guys provide a compelling touchstone for the children's desire to feel bigger, stronger, more powerful, and more certain of their agency and goodness.

Generating a Bad Guy Lexicon

Like any thorough investigation, this one requires some background research, what Pam calls "image searching." We hope to better understand the children's individual and collective conceptions of badness, so we can see more clearly what questions and offerings might be useful in challenging and expanding that thinking. In particular, we need to figure out what we might offer the children in groups, so that they can test their ideas with each other, draw inspiration from one another, and find their voice and power as a collective engaged in research together.

I comb through the year's dictated stories, drawings, pretend play transcriptions and transcribed conversations, literally collecting the ideas kids have posited over the course of the last few months about the nature of bad guys and their "badness." This retrospective form of active listening will provide the basis of what is to become the children's shared "lexicon" of bad guy terminology.

To begin a conversation aimed at generating a shared understanding of who or what a Bad Guy is,

BECOMING BAD GUY RESEARCHERS

I bring these lists to a lunchtime conversation with the six older children who gather for lunch, conversation, and books every day. I say, "Researchers like us collect our thinking so they can study it together. That's why I wrote down everything you've already said about bad guys." I can tell they are pleased that I've been scouring their work with such seriousness. They listen to their own words with a lens both appreciative and critical, mixing their "Uh huhs" and "Yeahs" with an occasional clarification or addition.

Here is the Bad Guy Lexicon we collected (and regularly amended) with the children over the course of our research...

Who are bad guys?
- Robbers
- Monsters
- Pirates
- Darth Vader and Storm Troopers
- Some might be machines
- Lions, panthers, bears, foxes (sometimes)
- Zombies
- Hunters

What do bad guys do?
- Hurt people and kill people
- Take things from people and break people's things
- Are hungry. They eat people, anything, everything
- Are scary, mean and BIG. Have BIG muscles
- Boss people around
- Don't know they're bad— only we know they are bad
- Bury the Good Guys
- Steal babies and kill them (and sometimes give them back)
- Bite / have sharp teeth

What are bad guy skills?
- Fight with swords and guns and bombs and shields
- Crash people with monster trucks
- Make poison and other yucky things
- Trap people
- Trick people
- Jump over things and leap from a tree and land safely everywhere
- Make things be on fire
- Frown and growl and roar

What other ideas do we have about bad guys?
- They are tall grown-ups
- They do NOT get married
- They are on teams with other bad guys
- They get tired, and they like to sleep on hard beds, and they spit and snore when they sleep
- They don't want to be rubbed
- They hate to draw
- They grow from magic eggs that nobody made
- They were not bad guys when they were little, but they learned to be bad guys
- They are angry

Making Our Research Visible

Once the children are satisfied with these lists, we put them in a binder for easy reference. We will add to these lists now and then, and turn to them in our everyday conversations about the bad guys who appear in the children's stories and pretend play. The terms will also inform our conversations about bad guys in the stories we offer the children—"real life" stories about the assassination of Dr. Martin Luther King or the discrimination experienced by Wilma Rudolph—and "pretend" stories like *Abiyoyo*; *The Terrible Nung Guama*; *Harry and the Terrible Whatzit*; *My Father's Dragon*; and multiple interpretations of *The Three Little Pigs*, with all their interesting variations on the Big Bad Wolf.

Meanwhile, we reorganize our visual display space, which we've historically reserved for easel paintings, self-portraits, and photographs of Children First kids playing at the Eno River. Now these spaces reflect the new centrality of Bad Guy Research.

This is a big moment. Children First teachers decided some time ago that we would keep our walls simple, and focus our reflective documentation efforts on extensive individual portfolios. Our culture, our curriculum, and our practices prioritize the individual child, so it made sense for our documentation to do the same. Teachers who focus on the developmental trajectory and "life story" of the individual child don't create bulletin boards about "what we are studying."

> But in this moment, we are a collective of Bad Guy Researchers; we—12 children, two teachers, one group—truly ARE studying bad guys.

Bad Guys Making Traps

Finn and Oliver Are Monsters in Their Hideout with Beds. They eat sticks! And when they sleep, they snore & spit.

Posting documentation about that work is not an empty gesture from some Reggio handbook; it's an authentic expression of who we really are.

So we post our lists of terms and our research questions about Bad Guys, along with the children's drawings and stories about Bad Guys, and photographs of Bad Guy play—all to create more accessible points of reference to inform conversation. In making the Bad Guy Research so visible—so fully public—we claim our emerging identity as Teacher-Researchers. For me and Sarah, there is something bold and unapologetic about making the choice to privilege this new content in our limited display space. And the shift away from featuring samples of individual children's expression to highlighting our collective work reflects a slow but seismic shift in the Children First culture. The Group—that long-neglected "13th child"—has found a place of honor.

CHAPTER 4

ACTION TO SUPPORT OUR RESEARCH

To complement and deepen our work on developing a shared terminology about the nature of bad guys and badness, Pam thinks we need to do something in a more visual language, to create, literally, a "shared image." The kids have already been drawing bad guys on their own, exploring their individual imagery. Now we are interested in what consensus they have achieved in their mental imagery. She offers us an approach that we've never tried before: a practice she calls "Shared Drawing."

In a shared drawing, the children direct the teacher as she draws on a surface that everyone can see: "Let's draw a bad guy together. You tell me how to draw it, and I'll hold the pen." Pam emphasizes that I should ask the children to be quite specific. If they say, "Draw a head" I should say, "What shape? Where? How big?" That way, the children understand that the marks I make are *their* ideas appearing on the page. Pam says, "As the children direct you, they are co-constructing a shared image. And you are gaining an understanding of what they all agree a bad guy is. Their symbolism should give a lot away."

This suggestion lands well for me; it seems doable and concrete, and it sounds like fun. I do pause to consider how this practice might bump up against a "rule for teachers" I've followed as long as I can remember, the one that says "Never draw for children." I imagine how it might feel to be a little flexible, to let that particular "sacred cow," as a past co-teacher once said, "run loose in the field." I remind myself that my genuine intention to support the children's research is more important than any particular practice used to manifest my intention. Ultimately, I'm glad to locate a willingness to relax and experiment and be a learner, knowing that I have the solid support of Pam and Sarah.

Creating a Shared Drawing

So, one morning late in January, I invite a group of six older kids to the work table in the tiny library building situated in the middle of our playground. They find seats and chat with one another as they watch me pin a large piece of white paper up on the wall.

Donna: So I'm wondering if it might be interesting to draw a bad guy together. I'll hold the pen, and you'll tell me what to draw.
Avery: A shooter.
Parker: No, a head, a head. Draw the body first. They're made out of bodies; it would be easier if she did a body first.
Donna: OK. What shape is the body?

And so we begin to create a visual image of a Bad Guy, as the children dictate one important feature after another...

- No smiles, since it's a bad guy.
- Zig zag teeth, in a mouth that's straight and grrrr.
- Scary eyes that are skinny and squinty, with dark pupils.
- A triangle nose, with no nostrils, because bad guys breathe in and out with their mouth.
- Skinny arms, and five hands, and four fingers on each hand.
- A shooter! Like a L shape, with a blower in it, and a trigger.
- A blue belt, with lots of buckles, to hold stuff like his shooter and his sword.
- A shield, with a picture of a dragon.
- Thick legs! But small feet.

The children lead from beginning to end, coming to an easy consensus about when the drawing is complete. When it's done, they sit for a moment and consider what we've made, clearly pleased. They decide that we should hang the Bad Guy on the outside library wall where he will overlook the playground. I'm still stapling the drawing into place when the cry goes out: "There's a monster coming! Run!"

And with that, the children launch into play, first battling this new Bad Guy, then becoming Bad Guys themselves, exploring Badness from both sides—perpetrator and victim.

When I later transcribe the dialogue and play, I notice that the children are grappling with some key issues. Is the Bad Guy a robber or a monster, or something else altogether? Is it a boy or a girl? Does the Bad Guy look silly, or scary, or "just weird?" It seems to me that rather than RESOLVING our diverse ideas about badness—boy vs. girl, real vs. pretend, robber vs. monster, silly vs. scary—this odd figure EMBODIES those tensions. Maybe that's why we all found him so satisfying. There was a palpable feeling of celebration, excitement and delight in that exercise of collective creation.

Documenting the work, I feel it all over again. There was such sweetness in the children's honesty about my clumsy drawing, their blunt commentary couched in genuine encouragement and consideration of my feelings. Maybe kindness was a by-product of the flow and togetherness in this work. I was helping the children do something together that none of us could do alone. I felt the zippy energy of co-construction during this experience, and it was exhilarating. The sense of being ONE group—that entity we have begun calling "the 13th child"—was fully present. And I was included in that collective, because my agenda was so fully aligned with the agenda of the group, which was at the same time so fully aligned with what Pam calls the "intention" of the individuals—their deep questions, concerns, and motivation.

Inviting the Bad Guy into Stories

Right away, the "Library Bad Guy" becomes a character in our lives, a handy and flexible foil for the children's pretend play. An exercise that began as a way to simplify, streamline, and clarify a collective image of badness turns out to be a shared platform for exploring badness in a more complex way. The children's relationship with the Library Bad Guy evolves over time, but the complexity is there from the beginning, as his creators waffle between seeing him as "scary" and finding him "silly." Likewise, he is sometimes "alien" and "enemy"' and other times, he is OUR Library Bad Guy, worthy of empathy, concern and care.

To find out more about how each of the children see and relate to the Library Bad Guy, I invite them to tell stories that include him as a character. This is a natural and comfortable provocation to offer, because storytelling is an established part of our weekly routine. We use a storytelling practice adapted from the work of Vivian Paley: the child speaks a story to a teacher, who writes it down just as the child tells it, and then reads it back so that the child can make corrections or additions as needed. After many years of using and refining this practice, we have come to see that telling stories is a fundamental human need, and that story work allows children to access and give form to the same compelling themes that animate their pretend play: love and power; safety and danger; fear and courage; silliness and magic.

Typically, I meet up with storytellers on the outside deck steps; in challenging weather, we meet at a table indoors. Either place, kids come one at a time, sometimes on their own, sometimes at my invitation; they pull their story journals out of the basket; and then they sit down beside me as I thumb through to the next blank page. Pen poised over paper, I say "Ready!" and the storyteller is off. At the most, I may offer a prompt like "What's going to happen in your story today? I can't wait to hear."

But today, I spread a blanket on the playground mulch so that the storyteller and I face the library. Our unusual location makes it easy for me to bring each storyteller's attention to the big bad guy drawing in front of us. Opening the journal to the first blank page in the usual way, I point to the library and say, "So, there's your character... What's going to happen?"

This change represents a small but potent shift in my role. Here, I am a provocateur, not simply repeating a familiar routine, but tapping into the power of that routine for research, my own and the children's.

ACTION TO SUPPORT OUR RESEARCH

The provocation turns out to offer a just-right balance of novelty and familiarity for both me and the children. We're comfortable AND excited, and the results are diverse and interesting. I notice that many of the children choose to linger on the blanket while their friends tell their stories, or stop by to listen on their way from one place to another. This is an individual activity, but perhaps because it's focused on a shared creation—the Library Bad Guy—it feels more like an activity we are doing as a group.

The stories shine a light on what the children make of—and what they CAN make of—the Library Bad Guy. They put him to use in many different ways...

For instance, in some of the stories, the Library Bad Guy is more naughty than sinister; he's a part of a team, or he eats dinner. In these examples, I sense the way that the storytellers identify with the bad guy.

Here, Aiden's priority for the Bad Guy— who he calls a "monster giant"— is much like his own priority at school these days— finding playmates among the older children. And in his happy ending, his bad guy finds not just one, but two powerful friends— a lion and a "bigger giant."

EATING // A Story by Aiden
Told on the playground looking at the Library Bad Guy on 02.02.17

Once there was a giant and it was a monster. And then it fights people. And then it started to eat and read something. And then he went outside to fight some more. And then he found a lion and he said, "Come with me and fight with me." And then he found a stone that he might want to throw somewhere. And then there was a bigger giant came and pushed the giant away. He wants to be on the lion's and giant's team. And then they started eating.

Like Aiden, Parker gives the bad guy a playmate. Although the monster duo "kills" the person, there is no real sense of menace in this short and snappy argument for the power of outnumbering your opponent.

> **MONSTER** // A Story by Parker
> Told on the playground looking at the Library Bad Guy on 02.02.17
>
> Once upon a time, there was the monster. And then he found another monster. And they played. Then they found a person and they fight the person. Cause there's two monsters, the person died.

Avery sets most of his stories in sports arenas, and his bad guy story is no exception. The badness here—disrupting a football game—is more annoying than frightening; in fact, it's a behavior Avery has likely encountered on our playground. And in the end his bad guy is just like a regular grown-up heading home to his chicken dinner.

> **BAD GUY** // A Story by Avery
> Told on the playground looking at the Library Bad Guy on 02.02.17
>
> The robber went to a football game. And then the robber saw a football and he took it since he's a bad guy and takes things that aren't his because robbers are mean bad guys like pirates. Then he goes back to his house and then he eats dinner. The End.
>
> *Donna:* What are bad guys' favorite foods?
> *Avery:* Chicken.
> *Donna:* And what's the size of the bad guy robber?
> *Avery:* Like a grown-up.

ACTION TO SUPPORT OUR RESEARCH

In other stories, the Library Bad Guy is downright terrifying, and his badness goes completely unchecked…

Sam's robber steals someone's shirt—a very personal assault— then adds further insult when he cuts the shirt up and puts it on his own bad body. The victim cowers in a blanket, realizing that she will never be able to wear her shirt again. Then the robber, in true bully fashion, breaks someone else's glasses. The best the victims can do to defend themselves is to throw the rest of their belongings at the robber—leaving them more exposed than ever.

ROBBER // A Story by Sam
Told on the playground looking at the Library Bad Guy on 02.02.17

Once upon a time, there was a robber. And it stole someone's shirt. And then he [the robber] cut the shirt and put it on. And it fit all the way down his whole entire body. And then it broke the glasses that it stole from another person. And then a blanket covered him. And then the person [whose clothes it took] put it on top of him because it was her clothes—she wants them back but he already cut a hole in it. And then someone threw a box on top of his head and they were his glasses. And they both threw their stuff that was on their bodies at him. The End.

Elisabeth's title "Too Late" captures perfectly the serial devastation wreaked by this bad guy arsonist, who keeps one house burning for so long that the firefighters cannot get away to stop any other fires.

TOO LATE // A Story by Elisabeth
Told on the playground looking at the Library Bad Guy on 02.02.17

Once upon a time—this is gonna be a scary story!—a bad guy came. And the bad guy tried to hit a house. And then a fire truck with a siren came, because the house was on fire [from the bad guy]. And then he really wanted to keep hitting the house to keep it fired so the fire truck would not get to any other fires. And then one time the fire stayed. And the bad guy was wondering how it was staying. Since it was going so long he didn't want it to go out. And suddenly the house got out of fire. And the house came back on fire because it was too late.

ACTION TO SUPPORT OUR RESEARCH

Some of the storytellers focus on conquering the bad guy.

Facing the Library Bad Guy from the safety of his cardboard box, Finn makes the bad guy a "hunter" who eats a deer after he stabs it with his spiky stick. But in his complicated scheme to get back at the hunter, Finn has sneaky people hiding "tags" and "powder sugar boxes" inside the deer—and that turns out to be very bad for the hunter. In the end, the hunter is gone, and only the people are left.

DEER // A Story by Finn
Told on the playground looking at the Library Bad Guy on 02.02.17

The character is a hunter.

Donna: Is a hunter a bad guy?
Finn: Yes.

The deer came. Then the hunter stabbed the deer with his stick that had little spikes on it. And then he [the hunter] ate it [the deer]. But then he [the hunter] died. Because it [the deer] was made out of tags on the inside; there were people hiding down below it so it was like tags on the inside. The tags were on a box full of powder sugar. The tags are bad for you and the box is bad for you too, but the powder sugar is not bad for you. Then the people were only left.

In a theme we will see often during the Bad Guy Research, Lia gives us a bad guy who is voraciously hungry. Opposite this predatory bad guy, she places a rabbit—the sort of small furry hero she likes best in her stories. This seemingly vulnerable character turns out to be powerful enough to stop a bad guy who has already eaten a whole house of chocolate and a whole apple.

THE BAD GUY // A Story by Lia
Told on the playground looking at the Library Bad Guy on 02.02.17

Once upon a time, a bad guy saw a rabbit. And then he saw chocolate and he could not eat because there was a caterpillar in the chocolate. And then he went and found a house that was full of chocolate. And then he ate it all until it was gone and he was still hungry. And then he ate a whole apple and he was still hungry. And then he saw the rabbit again and he tried to eat the rabbit but the rabbit kicked him until he died.

And some of the children show us another way to handle a bad guy: transformation. Forget being bad—there's so much fun to be had in this world! Let's find a friend, play family and stomp in puddles.

DINOSAUR & MONSTER // A Story by Mical
Told on the playground looking at the Library Bad Guy on 02.02.17

One day there was a monster and the monster said to the dinosaur, "Monster, let's play Family!" And then it starts to rain and stops raining. And then there was muddy puddles like this much. And then they jump up and down, and that's the end.

ACTION TO SUPPORT OUR RESEARCH

But it is Oliver, the youngest and most volatile Children Firster, who humanizes the Library Bad Guy in a way that takes my breath away. Oliver begins his story with loud sounds and fierce gestures, which I translate into "Once upon a time, there was a bad guy who was frowning and growling really loudly." Then he begins to speak in words: "He's growling at people that are mean." I say, "It sounds like he's really mad. What's he so mad about?" Oliver answers, "He's mad that he doesn't have any chocolate candy. He ate his candy. He's crying; he still can roar." I think for a moment about recent occasions when Oliver himself has literally "stolen" treats off other children's lunch plates, and snuck into his pantry at home to do the same. I say, "Wow, that Bad Guy is sad AND mad. I wonder what would happen if someone just gave him some candy." Oliver looks at me—full eye contact—then jumps up and runs to the Library Bad Guy, holding his hands up as if making an offering. I say, "You gave him some candy, Oliver! I wonder what he said." Oliver answers, "He said welcome, thank you for the candy." Even now, reading this story for the twentieth time, Oliver's gesture of monster-care—really a gesture of self-care—brings tears to my eyes.

Watching for Bad Guys in Pretend Play

As we move further into Bad Guy Research, we remind ourselves that we aren't steering toward some lesson that we want the children to learn about Bad Guys; in fact, we're not directed towards any endpoint or pre-determined destination. Nor do we set out with a list of activities in mind: *write stories, do self-portraits, add props, make the play visible*. We simply resolve to engage with the children around Bad Guy content in myriad ways, open to any possibility so long as it is grounded in our fundamental values of respect and trust. We'll try something, then pay attention to what happens: Is there excitement? Energy? Connection? Juice? Does what we're doing right now *feel* important, interesting, aesthetically satisfying? We will invent our way as we go, like scientists who experiment, observe the results, theorize, and experiment again.

And as we experiment in this way, attending to the subject of Bad Guys *alongside* the children, we also pay attention *to* the children. And what are we watching for, exactly? Pam speculates that our alignment with the children's concerns about badness—along with their own work on this subject—will operate together to move them toward more intellectual clarity and emotional security.

> In other words, it's possible that our presence and our sensitive attention, in and of themselves, may have a more profound impact on the children than any particular pedagogical offering we invent along the way.

And as we pay attention, there's one thing we notice right away. Even as we make more space in our days for conversation, drawing, building, and storytelling about bad guys, it's child-directed pretend play that continues to be the dominant pastime and expressive language of the children.

This makes sense. Pretend play is children's primary research *method*; it's how, as individuals and groups, they live into and explore the ideas and feelings they find most pressing and captivating. And for teachers, pretend play is a primary *subject* of research; we observe and, when we can, document the play, because the play is a window into children's thinking and emotional landscape. Children's pretending is rich with hints about what worries them; what frustrates them; what they long for; and what brings them joy. And that's especially true when pretending allows the children to BECOME the badness.

We see the children's sense of empowerment as they embody the compelling capabilities they attribute—not exclusively, but particularly—to Bad Guys: speed, size, strength, trickiness and teamwork.

We notice that some of the less desirable behaviors children ascribe to bad guys are more extreme versions of the mistakes they sometimes make themselves. These are the sorts of bad guy behaviors Avery calls "disgusting and naughty"—making messes, snoring and spitting, eating gross stuff, bathroom transgressions, taking things just because you want them. "Being" this kind of badness is almost like revisiting your less mature self, taking a vacation from your heroic everyday effort to behave in ways that adults deem acceptable.

And then there are bad guy behaviors that feel real world and quite scary: robbing, kidnapping, hurting, killing. These are bad guys breaching basic boundaries of safety; bad guys, the children worry, who may be more than "just pretend." "Being" this sort of badness may create a more comfortable and less vulnerable way to step close to that worry, and to explore the push and pull between being the aggressor or the victim, the winner or the loser, the powerful or the weak.

And of course, that tension is not merely theoretical. These intense children—each grappling with longing, worry, ambition and love—live this tension every day as they struggle to live safely and wholeheartedly in community with each other and with us.

> They may play at being the badness, but there is nothing make-believe about their quest to grow into being good "for real."

And really, it's the same for us teachers. We've been at it longer, but we too fear the real badness out in the world; and we too are humbled and challenged by the badness within ourselves as we try to grow toward being the good people we hope to be. And we're deeply curious about the children's journeys—individually and collectively—as they travel back and forth between being the badness and becoming good.

Because they experience the way we talk about and document their pretending, the children at our school know that we see their play as intrinsically important and interesting, and that, whatever our personal beliefs, we are open-minded about the content of that play. For example, neither Sarah nor I own guns, approve of corporal punishment, or support the death penalty. But we have always listened raptly to descriptions of weapons built from brio mechs and cardboard tubes; helped children tell and act their stories about killing bad guys; and transcribed pretend play in which "bad babies" are subjected to all kinds of good-natured torture. We don't try to talk the children out of the violence and into a more empathetic stance. We all know the difference between what's OK in pretending and what's OK in real life. Our intuition tells us to stand firmly in acceptance—really, in celebration—of the many ways children play at being the badness. We communicate that trust and acceptance through the way we observe, document and facilitate the children's forays into badness, and also through the opportunities we offer to extend those explorations.

The children also know that, while our stance about the content of play is relaxed and accepting, our insistence on physical and emotional safety in the play is fierce and unequivocal. As we position ourselves, literally and figuratively, just outside the bubble of the play, we act as advocates and coaches who make sure that the play is consensual and inclusive. We're there to remind kids to "let your friends know what you need" and to "ask first" and to "find a way that all can play."

We've always taught this way, but the Bad Guy Research moves our acceptance and advocacy for children's play from instinctual to conscious, and keeps our attention grounded in the specifics of this theme and how the children are working with it. The intentionality of the researcher's lens reminds us who we want to be as teachers—respectful, committed, and on the children's team. Not surprisingly, we find that now we enjoy and appreciate their play more than ever.

A Pretending Game about Badness

Take this typical example of a teacher offering support in the flow of play, helping with issues of consent, physical safety, and keeping agreements. Sarah captured this game with her recorder and camera, anticipating that it would hold riches for our Bad Guy Research as well as providing a snapshot of individual children at this moment in time.

This game starts late in the morning on the bike deck, where several kids are hanging out in that somewhat unorganized state of play that happens "between games." Then...

Finn: I'm a monster.
Avery: I'm a monster!
Mical: I am the monster. There can only be one monster. Because in one place there's just one monster. You cannot all be monsters!
Finn: I am and I have 1, 2, 3, 4, 5, five eyes!
Mical: Miles! Do you want to play our game?
Miles: Ya mean, catch Oliver?
Mical: Yes. We are playing monster and run to catch Oliver. Want to play?
Miles: Okay! (Enthusiastically)
Mical: Come on, let's go!

Now comes an important moment. The idea for this game centers on Oliver, the young friend whose reliable willingness to "be the enemy" is such a gift to these players. But even Oliver gets a choice, and no one has actually asked him yet.

Oliver is sitting quietly in the middle of the bike deck as the kids approach; they run at him, trying to initiate chase, but he's sitting still in an intentional and conspicuous way. Sarah reminds him to give the other kids the information they need about what he wants.

Sarah: Oliver, let them know if you're taking a break.

Oliver: I'm taking a break.

The kids back up and Oliver—in true tricky bad guy fashion—leaps suddenly to his feet and starts running, racing away as the other children jump into the chase.

Parker: (calls out as she runs) Oliver, is break over?

Oliver: Yeah.

Parker: Okay, great.

Here, Parker demonstrates real care for Oliver, making sure that she is reading his body language accurately, and that he really is consenting to be their bad guy. A few minutes later, several kids are chasing Oliver when Parker interrupts the game to propose a change in her role.

Parker: I'm on your team, Oliver!

Parker's younger friend Avery immediately follows suit.

Avery: I'm on Oliver's team!

Parker looks frustrated, and retracts her plan.

Parker: I'm not on Oliver's team.

Sarah watches for a moment as the play grinds to a halt, while several of the kids shout about whether they are or are not on Oliver's team, with Parker looking increasingly unhappy. Sarah offers an empathic guess about Parker's feelings.

Sarah: Oh, Parker, are you wishing it was just you and Oliver and hoping the other kids would make a different choice?

Parker: Yeah.

As often happens when someone else "gets" what we are feeling, Parker is now able to move past her upset. When Oliver starts roaring and running again, Parker jumps back into play, too.

Parker: Yoo hoo, Oliver! Try to come get me!

Now Mical snags a set of keys from the prop shed and heads to the playhouse.

Mical: (to the group)
I have an idea. I can put the monster in the house and lock him with this keys!

And Miles introduces a new idea, too, with the help of our playground binoculars, which he's picked up along the way. He stops, raises the binoculars, and dramatically searches the playground for the bad guy.

About this time, Oliver, perhaps tiring from the pressure of being the bad guy that everyone else is chasing, begins to "shoot" at his pursuers with his hands and arms, sometimes getting quite close to their faces. Sarah steps in to slow the action and offers a reminder about a foundational agreement governing Children First

pretend play: "Ask before shooting." That is, before he shoots, Oliver will need to make sure the other kids are up for a game that involves weapons.

Oliver: I'm pretending…
Sarah: I know. And our agreement is, "Ask first."

Sarah reminds all the players that Creation Station (an area stocked with recycled materials) is open for prop making if they decide they do want shooters for their game. She knows that sometimes even a brief shift into settled work with materials can serve both the game—enriching the play, and the players—allowing them a little break from the emotional and physical intensity of the play. Oliver does not, however, accept her invitation this time.

Mical: Miles, you know mine idea?
Miles: What?
Mical: We can shoot the monster, and put him in the house and lock him!
Miles: That's great!

Oliver allows himself to get "trapped" in the playhouse, and then he escapes, again shooting at his captors. Soon Oliver is captured and trapped again, and again Mical pretends to lock the door with the big keys, yelling:

Mical: He cannot come never out!

But almost immediately, Oliver does escape again! In pursuit, Avery introduces another new idea.

Avery: Don't worry, Miles, I'll get him with my whiskers! I'm a panther!
Parker: I'm a panther too. I got him down!

Parker has her hands on Oliver. He has been grabbed and tackled many times now. He slips away yet again—he really is quite phenomenal at wiggling out of difficulty—and now Miles grabs him and brings him down.

Sarah stays close. We know this kind of rough and tumble play is important to the children, and we love the practice it gives them with figuring out their own boundaries and the boundaries of other children in the game. Without stopping the play, Sarah reminds the older boys to listen to Oliver if he says 'Get off!'

But he never does. Instead, he wriggles away once again and runs off laughing. And somehow he also comes away with the keys! He is justifiably delighted with himself for "winning" the game in a way that is also fun for his friends.

Making the Bad Guy Pretending Visible

The way that Sarah relates to this bad guy play is business as usual at Children First—a teacher tending to the safety of the group, and to the individual growth of each player. But the Bad Guy Research also brings some small but important shifts in our documentation practice. For one thing, we talk and think more about the play, both with each other and with Pam as our pedagogical companion. We also talk more often with the children themselves about the play. We continue to document the full range of their pretend games for portfolios, but now we also create small books and displays with captioned images of bad guy pretending, hoping to create more "buzz" about these games and about what children think and feel when they are playing them. We try to highlight the moments when kids use multiple languages—speaking, acting and making with various materials—to embody badness.

So, for example, we post small stories like these on a bulletin board by the snack table.

ACTION TO SUPPORT OUR RESEARCH

Miles and Avery built these bad guy weapons in the Creation Station, and got help from Parker and Sam to build their "lookout" with foam blocks.

Here, Miles and Avery have built their lookout with big blocks in the loft room, and their weapons are brio mech guns that shoot "Hot Lava Marshmallows."

Avery:	They're shooters.
Sarah:	Whoa. What comes out of yours?
Avery:	Foam balls. Like soft.
Miles:	Hard, metal bullets come out.
Avery:	Mine, I mean mine are hard.
Sarah:	So are you both bad guys in the game?
Avery:	Yeah. We're the robbers. Robbers are mean.
Miles:	And that's our lookout.

At the creek, bamboo is the loose part of choice. Here, Oliver, Maya and Mical, armed with bamboo swords and shooters, play a fierce game of Abiyoyo.

Occasionally, we were lucky enough to have an extra set of hands and eyes on the playground, and then we all—children and teachers alike—got to see the Bad Guy pretending documented through fresh eyes. Here's an example of pretend play reminiscent of the Poison Gatorade from the first day of school. At the Water Deck, bad guys are often busy mixing a terrifying array of lethal potions. Today, a visiting teacher watches as Parker and Elisabeth pour water into some cups and bowls while stirring shaving cream into others. Some younger kids come near, and ask a question, "What are we making?"

Elisabeth: We're making yucky ice cream for bad guys.

Their cheerfully diabolical energy is contagious. The players move quickly, selecting tools, pumping colored water, squirting more shaving cream, stirring with a fury, studying their results, broadcasting their progress, then arranging their products on various tables. They are giggling, but they are also business-like, productive.

Now Elisabeth and Parker decide to make a shift. They are no longer tricky good guys killing bad guys; they ARE the tricky bad guys.

Parker: Pretend we don't say it's for bad guys. We just say to everybody, "Yeah it's so good for you!"

Elisabeth: And when they swallow it, they die, right?

They explain that they are going to sell their poison ice cream to the "villagers"—the little people figures who come over asking for "pretty porridge." Elisabeth drops one figure into a cup overflowing with white fluffy water and says, "Ah, I died!"

Parker and Elisabeth continue dropping the villagers into the cups, then cough as if they are the villagers dying. They take the people figures out, dry them off, and drop them in again.

Each time one of the "villagers" walks up, the girls make them ask, "Can I have something to drink?" and then deliver their tricky answer: "Sure, it's very good for your body."

Later, debriefing her day with me and Sarah, the visiting teacher observes, "It is sanctioned meanness. Sanctioned trickiness. It is a time to practice doing something that you would never ever actually do to another person, and all with a smile on your face!"

CHAPTER 5

OFFERING MATERIALS FOR BAD GUY RESEARCH

Periodically during these months of bad guy research, we offer new materials for the children to use in their bad guy play. We think of these offerings as small queries in the larger research project. Will the children engage with these materials, and if so, how? Will they find them useful for bad guy study?

And what can we learn about the children's thinking and feeling as we watch their work with these materials?

Sometimes our offerings are simple. For instance, after clocks with "bad guy alerts" appear in some of the children's storytelling, we happen to end up with a broken clock in our collection of useful junk. One morning when I have time to watch the pretending, I place the broken clock in a conspicuous place on the playground. Early on, a small group of children gathers around to look it over and claim possession, but soon it is left behind, seemingly forgotten as the children pursue other possibilities.

Picking up the abandoned clock, I shrug philosophically. As Pam often reminds us, it's not unusual for some of the provocations we offer to be what I would call "flops." Not a problem, she says, as long as you listen closely enough to know when to shift or let go. The children will always come back, she assures us, to what's important.

Bad Guy Action Figures

Early every year, we print small full-body photographs of each Children Firster and their family members in an "action pose" of their choice; trim around the figures; laminate them; and place them in clear plastic stands that hold them upright. We call these "Family Action Figures,"

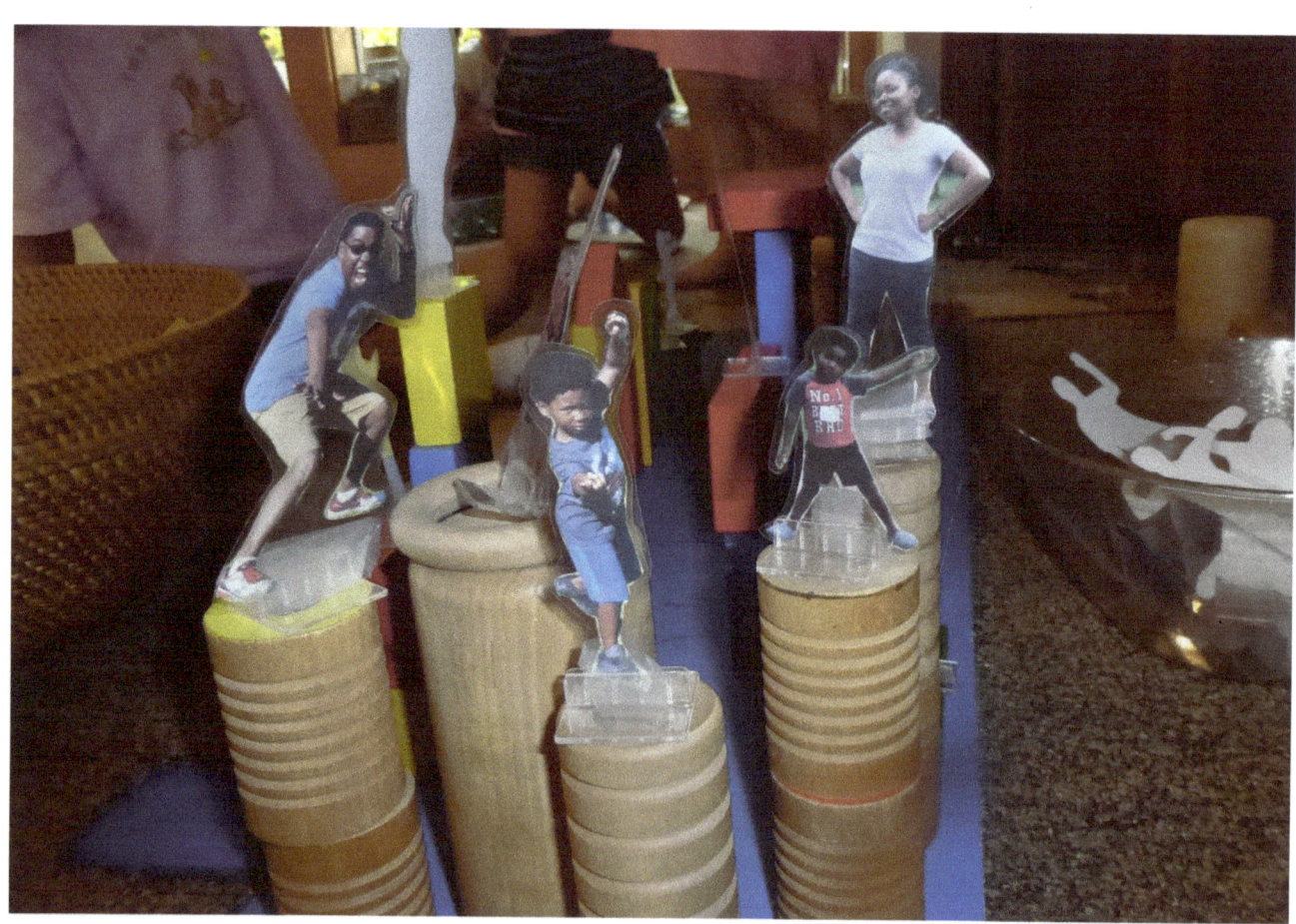

and the children use them daily in their block buildings and small scale pretending.

Now we wonder if the kids might find an adaptation of these familiar and beloved props useful for pretending about badness. So Sarah photographs each child in a "bad guy pose" and turns those photographs into new "Bad Guy Action Figures." Soon, the children are calling their original action figures their "Good Guys" and combining both sets of figures in their play.

Sometimes the Bad Guy Action Figures hang out in the block area with the Good Guys, and sometimes we bring them to a table we've set with interesting assortments of loose parts and builders. In the spirit of making our research visible, we collect children's work with the Bad Guy Action Figures in a little book.

Here are some examples of the ways children use these figures to show Bad Guy action, and, surprisingly often, to show Bad Guys connecting with one another. We know that play with the Family Action Figures is all about relationship, so perhaps we should have expected that the Bad Guy Action Figures would inspire play about relationship, too.

Finn, who in his real life at school is just beginning to move out of solitary activity into group play, uses the bad guy action figures to put himself in the very middle of the social action.

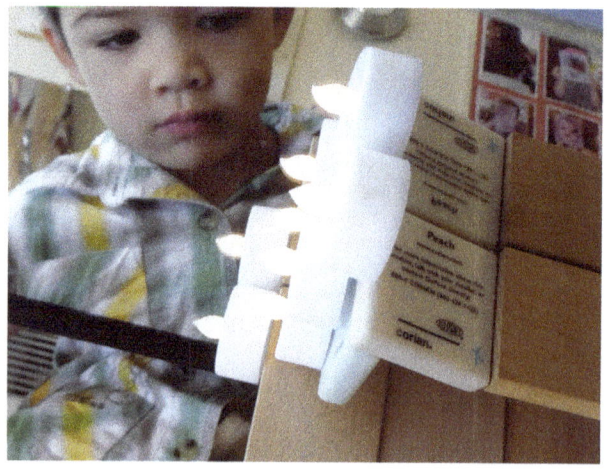

Donna: There are a lot of bad guys and you're in the middle of them. There are three on this side of you and three on that side. You look like you're on a team.

Finn: They're on a team.

Similarly, Miles has decided to create an inclusive and exciting scene for the bad guys. We especially enjoy his idea to use the battery-powered tea lights as flames coming out of the back of the rocket.

Miles: This is a rocket and all the Children Firsters are going to go in it.

OFFERING MATERIALS FOR BAD GUY RESEARCH

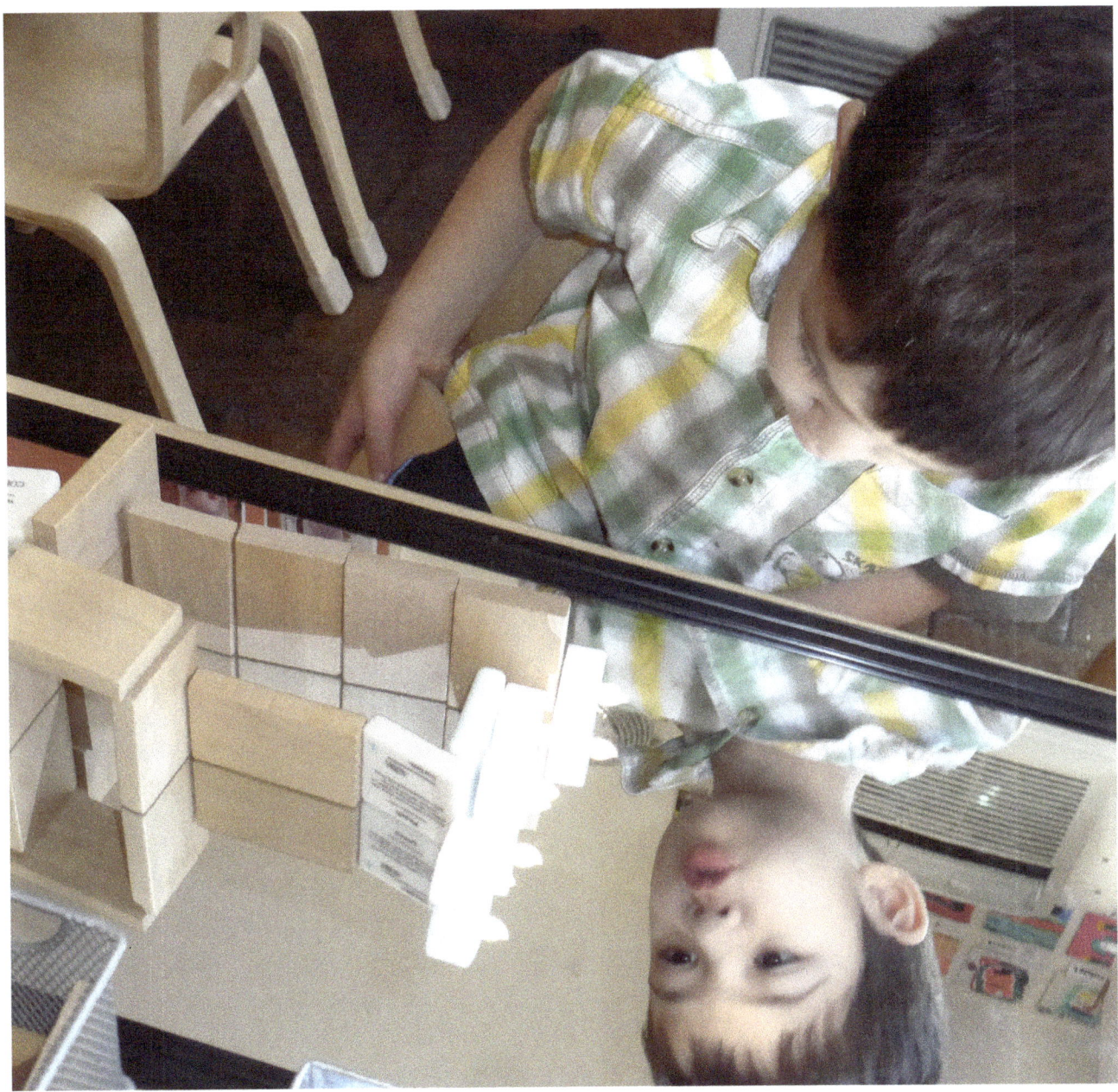

In fact, the tea lights often make an especially potent addition to the Bad Guy arrays. For Elisabeth, the lights are a source of tricky protection from the bad guys.

Elisabeth: Mine is where these mean guys are but no one can step in the fire. When they step in the fire, they die. They don't know that it's fire. They don't know it's real fire.

But here the play with tea lights takes a tender tone, as Mical identifies with and cares for the bad guys…

Mical: I turned off all the candles because I don't want the bad guys to get burned.

Bad Guy Self-Portraits

As we continue to look for ways to support the kids in "being the badness," we turn to the familiar practice of portrait-making. During one of Pam's visits, she and Sarah sit with kids at the drawing table and offer this invitation: "Draw yourself in real life and then draw yourself as a bad guy." Our intention is to give children a choice about whether and when to "be the badness"—we are supporting it, not promoting it! And we're curious about how they will render the relationship between their good guy and bad guy selves. The children's portraits,

we think, might offer a useful vantage from which to see their ideas about the *who* and *how* of goodness and badness.

The drawings are interesting in and of themselves. Aiden, for instance, says, "I just don't want to make myself into the bad guy." Instead, he exercises his artistic power to portray his older brother Alex as the bad guy. Sarah wonders if Alex will mind, and Aiden says, "I don't think so. He's just a little bigger than me." Big enough, perhaps, to shoulder the burden of the bad guy role.

A week later, I invite the kids to tell stories about their drawings. Later, we'll take these stories to meeting, where we'll make them into simple plays—another regular storytelling practice inspired by Vivian Paley. Sitting in a circle with the children, I read a story aloud, and the storyteller tells us which character they choose to be. Then I go around the circle, inviting each child to choose a different character to play, until all the roles in the story are filled. Children who don't end up with a part are the audience. The actors take their places, and I read the story once again, pausing as the actors show the action and deliver the dialogue. We learn a lot about children as we see which characters they choose to be, and how they embody those characters.

In fact, this whole process—creating the portraits, telling the stories, and acting out the stories—offers rich insight into the children's growing capacity to manage their own bad guy narratives. Although we expressly invite them to "draw yourself as a bad guy and a good guy," some of the children— like Aiden—choose to draw someone other than themselves in one role or the other. When they tell stories about those characters, they make another round of choices about who will "be the badness" and how that badness will present itself. And in the acting, the storytellers have yet another choice to make: among all the characters they've put in the story, who will they embody? When they make these choices, we see the children's power and fluency in "using" bad guy imagery for their own purposes; they are driving the narrative, not being driven by the narrative.

OFFERING MATERIALS FOR BAD GUY RESEARCH

Take Parker, for instance. Not only does she exercise her own right to choice in this activity, she respects other children's right to choose as well…

Sarah: Parker, now that you're finished with your self-portrait, would you like to draw yourself as a bad guy?
Parker: No, thank you.
Sarah: Do you want to take a break from drawing, or do you not want to show yourself as a bad guy?
Parker: I don't want to make myself into a bad guy.
Sarah: Is there someone else that you'd like to draw as a bad guy? Someone you know?
Parker: Finn?
Sarah: I wonder if that'd be okay with him. Do you want to go and ask him?

Parker goes off to ask, then comes back and lets Sarah know that Finn said no, but that Miles said yes.

And here's the story she tells later:

"Bad Guy Miles" by Parker
Once upon a time, there was Parker. And then a bad guy Miles came and fighted Parker. And they both had swords, shields and shooters and because there was more on Parker's team, the bad guy Miles died.

Donna: Who was on Parker's team?
Parker: My imaginary friends.
Donna: Was Bad Guy Miles alone or on a team?
Parker: He has only one person on his team and mine has ten.

When we act this story, I ask Miles to be himself, and to choose one person for his bad guy team—he chooses Sam. The rest of the kids line up with Parker. It makes the math of this story—a critical element—quite clear. I can see that Miles and Sam feel a bit uncomfortable as they embody the "outnumbered and defeated" storyline. Afterwards, I sincerely thank the two boys for being willing to take the "losing parts" in order to make the story acting happen.

When Alena tells her story, she elects to change the identity of her "good Alena" self-portrait into Wonder Woman. In this way, Alena herself becomes a character powerful enough to wrangle the monster version of Alena.

"Save" by Alena

Once upon a time, there was a monster. And then there is a person named…

(in this long pause, I ask "Wasn't that a self-portrait?" and she says, "Yes, but…" and I say, "Oh, do you have a plan to change the name?" and she says "Yes," then thinks a little more, then…)

…Wonder Woman. And then the monster looked around smelling Wonder Woman. And then the monster found Wonder Woman. And Wonder Woman took her rope and trapped the monster. And then she puts the monster in jail.

Naturally, when we act the story, Alena chooses the Wonder Woman role.

OFFERING MATERIALS FOR BAD GUY RESEARCH

Miles' work with this provocation goes directly to the question of real vs. pretend. He puts his bad guy self into dialogue with his real self, and the two come to a quick consensus: there is silliness here, but no real menace. When we act his witty rendition of bad guy silliness, Miles chooses to be the bad guy.

"Infinity" by Miles

Once upon a time, there was a nice guy that said [to the bad guy], "Are you being silly?" And the bad guy said, "Yes." And then the good guy says, "How silly are you?" And the bad guy says, "A million silly! Or infinity silly!" They play at each other's houses. The End.

PURSUING BAD GUYS

Elisabeth uses this exercise to work on managing suspense, a challenge she's been grappling with all year. In a lunchtime conversation just the week before, Elisabeth tells us she would rather have something scary BEHIND her so she doesn't know it's there. Now, in her drawing, Elisabeth does, indeed, put the monster behind her, and then renders herself as angry, animating herself with fierce emotion rather than running away or hiding from the threat. And in her story, she includes a truly horrific element—a monster hand rising from the floor—and elects to BE that scariness in acting the story.

"Stick Insect and Bad Guy" by Elisabeth

Once upon a time, there was an angry kid that was about to turn into a pirate. [She's angry because there's a monster behind her because she doesn't like the monster]. And then another pirate came and said "Arrrrgh." And then they both died, because they were really old. And then a stick insect came. And the stick insect magic-ed the dead pirates. And then they came back alive. They got rusted. And then they went home and they live together. And then a monster hand stuck out of the floor. They were scared and the hand grabbed one of the foot and they all died.

OFFERING MATERIALS FOR BAD GUY RESEARCH

Mical takes this opportunity to explore the real-life tension between the "bad" impulses she often struggles to manage and her desire to be powerful in a "good" way.

"Play Safely" by Mical

Once upon a time, there was Mical and a bad guy. The bad guy kick Mical. And she said, "No, go away!" And the bad guy did not listen. She hit him and she pushed him so he goes away, but he stays there the whole time. He was REALLY bad. Then he said, "Ok, I will go away for one minute and I will try not to kick you again." Then he came back and she said, "OK, I will not hit again and push you again." They're friends now because they're playing, "Can I have that when you're done?" They are playing safely.

I smile as I consider Mical's hopeful conclusion—"They are playing safely"—a declaration that could serve as a real-life happy ending for the big collective story we might title "Children Firsters Being the Badness."

CHAPTER 6

PROTECTION FROM BADNESS

Looking back, it's clear that there was a kind of Yin and Yang to the children's Bad Guy Research. Certainly, they found "Being the Badness" a thoroughly compelling way to live into questions like these: *If I'm bad, can I ever change to good? Who has more power, the bad guys or the good guys? Can my pretending trick you so you don't know if I'm bad or good?*

But even as they claimed the power to embody badness, they began to turn that growing power toward the possibility of "Stopping the Badness."

Early in the year, Sarah and I assumed that the children's pretending about badness was grounded in their longing for safety and clarity. We noticed the children's unusually fierce and intractable attitude about the trajectory of their Bad Guy storylines. When we asked about pretending games, the children reported, often in grim detail, their plan to KILL all the bad guys in the game. For example, during a game at the start of the year, Lia said "I'm glad Abiyoyo is dead!" I asked "Why, I wonder?" She responded, "So that he won't eat anybody." Her tone—"Isn't it obvious?"—communicated a compelling logic: When you get rid of the Bad Guy, you get rid of the bad things he does.

> When observing this sort of pretending, our long-held teaching practice had been to "complicate the play"—to invite more creativity and less violence, and to promote development of perspective-taking and empathy.

We would raise little questions here and there, inviting the children to think beyond what we saw as their understandable but primitive response to danger. Often we would ask "Why do you think the bad guy is doing that?" Or, "I wonder what's bothering him." This year, the answer was almost always, "Nothing. He's just BAD." Then we might say, "Well, I wonder if there's any way to change his mind. Maybe you could invent a way to change him to good?" Again, the answer would be "He is NEVER going to be good" or "He NEVER wants to be good." If preschoolers had the habit of rolling their eyes at adults, these children would have been rolling theirs at our ridiculous ideas about bad guy rehabilitation. They treated these inquiries as sentimental and silly at best, and more likely, a hindrance to important work that needed to be done. Badness is an absolute, they seemed to be saying, and as such, it must be banished thoroughly, immediately and permanently.

As we accompanied the children in their work as Bad Guy Researchers, we pulled back from our earlier ways of inserting ourselves into their play. Now we didn't need to complicate the play for the children; they were already engaging at a level of nuance and complexity that we'd not seen earlier in the year. Their play was changing, and perhaps the children were also expanding what they were willing to share with us, as we shifted from "teaching toward empathy" to journeying alongside them WITH empathy. They weren't rolling their eyes at us anymore, and we certainly weren't wishing they would "mix it up" in their play. Meanwhile, as Sarah and I got more alert and curious, the children got more interested in what we had to offer.

Pretend Play about Protection

Shortly after the arrival of the Library Bad Guy, for example, Finn brings the possibility of "making protection" to the playground pretending. He had initially integrated the Library Bad Guy into his habitual solitary pretending—creeping up on the picture, then dashing away, or "shooting" at it from a safe distance with a simple improvised weapon. But today,

Sarah notices that Finn is dragging some big blocks over to the mulched area in front of the library, and he tells her that he's "building a wall" to protect himself and the other kids from the bad guy. Sarah broadcasts his idea to other players, and soon he has a whole team working alongside him.

Almost every day, this Protection theme shows up somewhere at school. We see Finn and Oliver burying turtles in the rice table and lions in the sand river to "keep them safe." Elisabeth tells us about a water deck game when "me and Oliver and Mical were making yummy drinks for animals who are dead so they can come back alive." In the loft room, Elisabeth builds a police car fully stocked with food and flowers, which she uses to "pick up someone that did something bad."

Here a team of good guys—The Paw Patrol—protect themselves from bad wolves by pretending to be dead. I stop to ask about the game when I notice a whole line of children lying perfectly still along the top of a big block shelf on the playground...

Donna: I thought y'all were dead. I was a little worried.

Miles: No, what I was dying for was to trick the bad guys like they think we're really dead but we're not.

At a building table we have set up outdoors, Oliver and Elisabeth use small blocks to create enclosures that protect little frogs.

Oliver: That's the safe home, that's the safe home, that's the only safe home that he builded.... This is all my safe town there is.

Donna: You're so busy creating safety. You're like a protector for the frogs.

Elisabeth: The big bad wolf lives right there, and the little froggies every day when they get food, they come AROUND the big bad wolf.

Donna: They come around to avoid him. And is that working for them to stay safe that way?

Elisabeth: Uh huh, a little bit.

Donna: Are they nervous? You look nervous when you talk about it.

Elisabeth nods, but she is smiling.

Stories about Protection from Badness

In the stories that children told before embarking on Bad Guy research, they exhibited the same inclination we saw in their pretending—eliminate Bad Guys as quickly and permanently as possible. But as the research unfolds, Children First storytellers begin to claim a broader range of approaches to protecting themselves and others from badness.

One device is what we come to call "misunderstanding." In these stories, it turns out that what seems like badness at first is really not a problem at all. Here's an example from Lia...

"The Girl" by Lia

Once upon a time, she saw a lion. She got sad when she saw the lion. She tried to run away but it was too late because the lion already had grabbed her. But she realized the lion was nice; the lion wanted her to be his pet. And then the lion took her home and showed her to his Mom and Dad and also her brother and sister. Then she was happy.

When Oliver and Miles tell a partner story, they begin with the usual "kill the bad guy" storyline, but then friendship shifts the narrative ....

"The Big Chuck-a Cheese Monster" by Oliver and Miles

Oliver: There was a big chuck-a monster and a big chuck-a cheese that he's eating.

Miles: And then there's a nice guy that comes and kills the monster.

Oliver: And it comes alive and turns nice and they're best friends.

Miles: They all get guns and they shoot the clouds [just for fun]. All they shoot is fireworks.

Oliver: They eat two big chuck-a-cheese, because they're big kids.

We might call this solution to Badness "Joining a Team." The children know from their own experience that the attractions of Badness are no match for the magnetic force of friendship. And they seem to suspect that the worst badness is conceived and nourished in solitude.

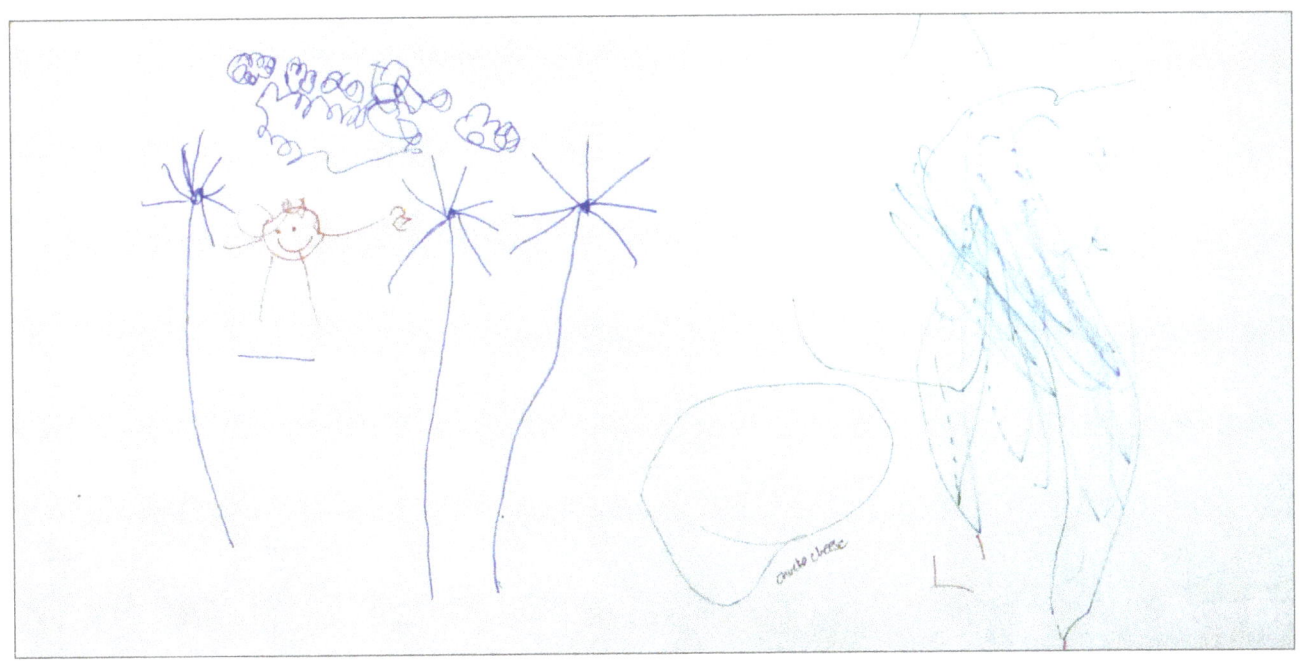

PURSUING BAD GUYS

When faced with badness that will not change, the children often call on "the police" to restore safety and order. Lia's relentlessly sinister rendition of Abiyoyo begins with a drawing in which she gives him two hearts—one that is still beating, and one that has stopped beating and that is the source of his badness. Then she gives him multiple bad guy behaviors—not just stomping and eating, but also stealing.

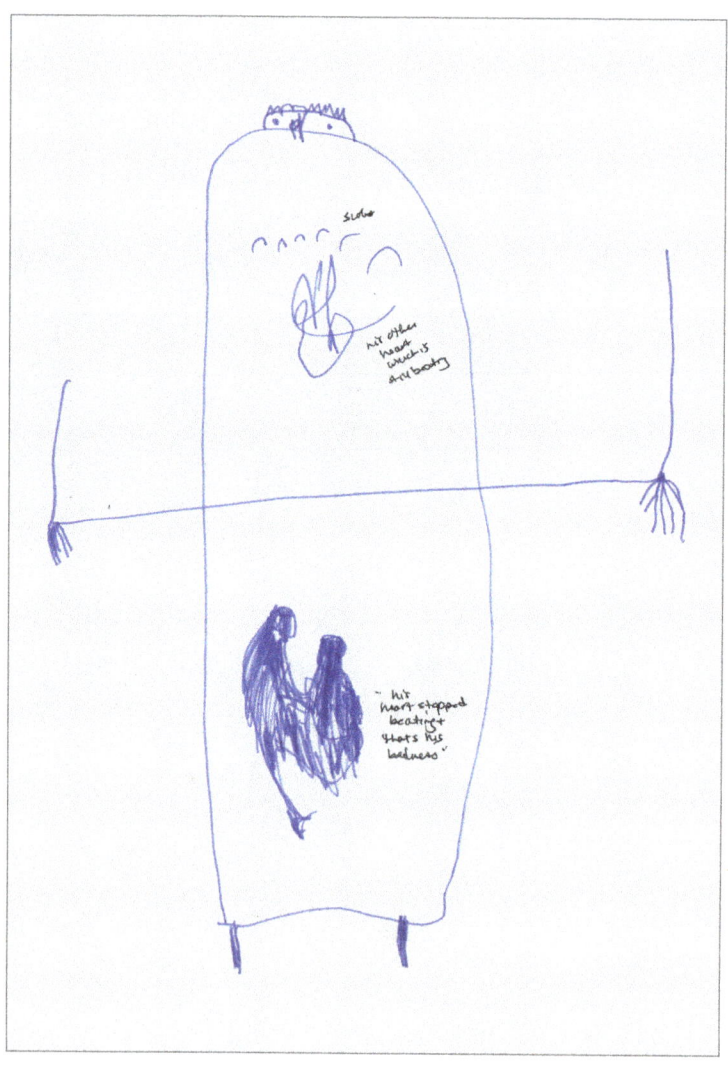

"The Bad Guy" by Lia
Once there was a monster named Abiyoyo and he stomped on a building. And then he stomped on a person and then ate the person. And then he ate a building and he ate some flowers. He took money from people. And then Abiyoyo stomped on a leaf that he saw and then he stomped on anything he saw except for other bad guys. Because he was the meanest bad guy of all. The End.

Donna:	Wow, Lia—so nothing stops all that badness, huh?
Lia:	Actually I'm not finished. And then he saw a mirror and he stomped on that mirror. That's the end.
Donna:	Whoa—so nobody IS going to stop him?

Lia: And then he went to jail; a police officer put him in jail because the police officer was too quick.

And of course, sometimes it's the child herself—or the character she chooses to play—who singlehandedly defeats the badness. Mical's Abiyoyo story is astonishing to me, intense and complete. There is a terrifying encounter with the monster; there is a Lion Daddy who comes to the rescue; and then there is a sort of epilogue in which the survivors relax in the safety of their home and process their traumatic experience through drawing. In a way, this storyline reflects the sort of processing we are doing collectively in our larger study of bad guys.

"Daddy Save Maya and Elisabeth" by Mical

One day… some persons hear a storm; Abiyoyo was pushing his feet onto the ground, stomping. Then Elisabeth and Maya came and said, "No!" because they have shooters and they shoot him and make him go away. But then he grabs them with both hands and tries to eat them—but my Daddy came and he was a lion and he grabbed Abiyoyo and he eats him! Then they celebrate and they eat cake. Then they went to the beach and build a sand castle and they draw in their house, papers of monsters.

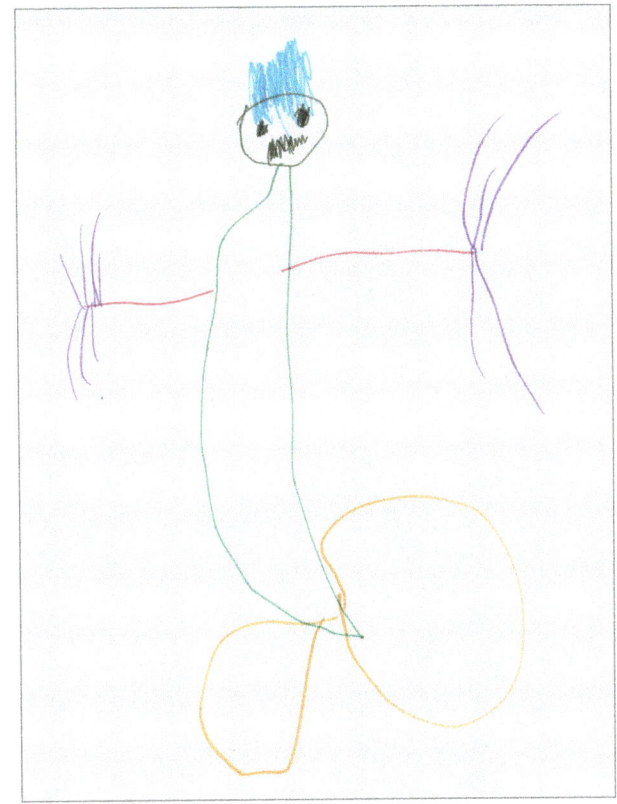

Mical's Abiyoyo

The Teacher's Role in Protection

In our many lunchtime conversations about bad guys, the older children come again and again to questions of "how to stay safe from badness." As their adult companion, this is tricky and tender territory for me. In my role as co-researcher, my preference is to keep the questions open and the conversation flowing, to ask clarifying questions and leave the children to settle on their own conclusions about what is true, what is real, what is possible, and, especially, how best to deal with the badness in the world. On the other hand, I am their caregiver, and I have a responsibility to offer a sense of security and to provide honest and reassuring information when they ask urgent and earnest questions about whether they are safe.

> Ideally, I will use the power of *my* role in the classroom to foreground *their* personal and collective power.

I want the children to know that they are strong individuals, and also that they are not alone. I believe that if adults help children root in the nourishing ground of community, the children will develop the hardiness and courage they need to reckon with the moral complexity and the danger in both their imagined worlds and the real world.

My aspiration is clear, but in the day-to-day reality of teaching toward that aspiration, I am often quite muddled. In this conversation about Martin Luther King, I feel the tension between the researcher role and the caregiver role quite keenly:

Elisabeth: If I was Martin Luther King and I saw a gun pointing at me, before the person shot me I would say "No."
Parker: But it happened very quick, he didn't have time.
Miles: You wouldn't have time because they really come out really fast. As fast as a rocket.
Parker: Or as fast as a lightning. You can't have time to answer.
Elisabeth: OK.
Miles: Just run away from it.
Elisabeth: OK.

Parker draws on her memory of an image from a book about Martin Luther King that showed him lying on a balcony after he was shot...

Parker: But he couldn't—there was just a little space, he was on a little deck, he didn't have space, he couldn't run away or jump down from the deck, from his hotel and run away.
Donna: Maybe if he knew someone was going to shoot at him he would have laid down flat.
Miles: When the bullets are coming he should have dived down really fast.

Sam: Or I guess he could just jump onto a car and then climb into it.

Parker: But people were behind him so maybe they would get shot.

And here we are, together in uncertainty: maybe there really wasn't a way for Martin Luther King to keep himself safe, and maybe there was. As I hold the tension between being a co-researcher and a caregiver, I tune myself to the children's energy. The children are winding down into a low hum of sadness and resignation; we are sitting together with the truth that hard things happen. I could say something reassuring like "Knowing how quick y'all are, I bet you would have figured out a way to move." Or "Good thing that the person who shot Martin Luther King is not around anymore, huh?" But in this moment, I intuit that it's more important to offer something more basic—the example of a fellow human sitting humbly and quietly with the complex, achy truth: It's hard, it's sad, AND we're OK. Offering simple presence feels consistent with the general message we aspire to communicate in the Bad Guy Research: "We're in this WITH you." Not shrinking from hard and scary things, and not unmoored by them either. Turning toward.

And the kids, in this moment, seem able to settle themselves for a moment or two, breathe through their worry, and move on.

A Provocation about Protectors

Our pedagogical guide, Pam, is scheduled to visit again in early March; it's been about a month since her work with Sarah and the kids on their bad guy self-portraits. We have a clear idea of what we'd like from her this time. We ask her to step into the work as if *she* were the classroom teacher in the midst of this research. In particular, we're hoping she will lead our whole-group meeting—a setting that she believes is ripe for more research-focused conversation.

I'm not sure I agree with Pam about whole-group conversation. I have a deep-seated aversion to meetings (for children *and* adults) where too many people are competing for airtime. Asking young children for a lot of listening and waiting strikes me as a recipe for restlessness and misbehavior. At Children First, we've settled on a plan for the day that includes just one group time—our noon Meeting. We've learned that after a full morning of work and play, especially with lots of time outdoors, the children are more than ready to sit together for half an hour while I "hold the space" and lead activities.

In our Meeting routine, we sing everyone's name; check in about friends who are absent; call "old friends" and family members for their birthdays; talk about what will happen tomorrow and the next day, and count "how many days" until upcoming events we are excited about. The rest of the half hour flies by as we act out the children's dictated stories; sing and dance; and hear the latest "Friend Doll News"—persona doll stories about social dilemmas and ethical challenges like "respect bugs" and "find a way that all can play" and "how to be safe when you're really, really mad."

Pam sees the value in all of this "ritual and protocol." At the same time, she remains convinced that more whole group conversation about the children's research will further their shared work and strengthen the identity of the collective, that important "13th child." I'm skeptical, but also curious. What might a group conversation look like if it is focused on subject matter that genuinely matters to the children? Pam agrees to offer a demonstration, and comes prepared with a provocation.

I open meeting in the usual way, then turn things over to Pam. We record the conversation so that we can study it later, to learn from Pam's example, and to think about possible next steps. The conversation, excerpted here, lasts a full 10 ½ minutes.

Pam: I was so interested to see when I came back that your bad guy on the library was still there. And he was making me think about other bad guys that are on buildings. Ever seen a bad guy on a building before?
Many: No.
Pam: Let me show you some, and then I have a surprising piece of information for you.

Pam shows a picture.

Pam: What's that?
Aiden: Lion.

Pam:	That one?
Parker:	That? Monkey.
Finn:	Gargoyle!
Pam:	How did you know?!
Finn:	**Because it looks like a gargoyle.**
Pam:	You are so right—it is a gargoyle, Finn. Does it look like a bad guy?
Many:	Yes.

Next picture…

Miles:	Dragons.
Parker:	Bears?
Lia:	Monster.
Sam:	Zombies?
Maya:	Dogs.
Pam:	Finn, do you know where gargoyles go?
Mical:	Schools.
Parker:	**On churches.**
Pam:	Or castles.
Elisabeth:	Castles?!
Pam:	All of these are on the buildings they're on, or in front of the buildings they're in front of, for the same reasons. To protect the building.

PROTECTION FROM BADNESS

Parker:	How?
Miles:	To scare the people that might break in.
Sam:	So creatures don't make holes inside their buildings.
Elisabeth:	And so woodpeckers won't peck on their houses.
Mical:	And so birds don't eat someone's food.
Pam:	There's a lot of things they can protect against. But I was wondering if there's any possibility that your library bad guy could also be a protector.
Elisabeth:	He protects the library so nobody opens the library and takes all our stuff home.
Miles:	He's not that scary to me: he looks funny.
Elisabeth:	He looks funny, weird, interesting and silly.
Oliver:	But the house can keep him really safe from the big giant monster.
Pam:	You think you need another protection? You need the bad guy, but you also need another protection?
Oliver:	Yeah. I need a gargoyle and a big monster to protect the library.
Pam:	Do you all agree?
Many:	Yeah!
Sam:	I think they should be all over the library.

Elisabeth:	No, I think they should be all over the playground.	Sam:	A wooden bad guy.
Miles:	I think we should cut the Library Bad Guy out, and make it scarier. It's just paper, it looks like pretend... but if you cutted it out, it will look scarier.	Miles:	Clay maybe?
		Sam:	Clay, and then you could fire it.
		Pam:	Then it could stay outside forever, right? How big would these statues have to be?
Pam:	All of these that I've shown you are photographs, so they're on paper right now, but in real life, they are what Miles is saying—three dimensional. They're statues. So are you thinking that you would make the bad guy on the library now into a statue? Is that what you said, Miles? I'm checking in.	Many:	Big, huge!
		Pam:	Do you have enough clay for that?
		Many:	No!
		Miles:	Maybe we can get a million pieces of clay, like all the clay at the store and bring it over here.
		Parker:	Maybe we should get some playdough to add the colors and then we should get some clay...
Lia:	I like that idea.	Donna:	You can actually add color to clay, Parker; you've done it before. Do you remember how?
Sam:	I love that idea.		
Miles:	Maybe someone—one of my friends—could carve one out.	Elisabeth:	Glaze!
Pam:	Make a bad guy like the one on the library but have it carved?		
Miles:	Yeah.		
Pam:	How else could you make something like that, a statue bad guy, how could you make that three-dimensional?		

The conversation continues a bit longer, and ends with a strong collective sense of "Yeah! Let's do this!"

What a rich offering Pam has made. For me and Sarah, she has demonstrated that a whole group conversation can zoom along with that same rising energy and collective momentum that we are learning to watch for in small group work. And through Pam's skillful and even-handed facilitation, we see more clearly the capacity of younger and quieter kids to make a significant contribution to the group.

In re-listening to and transcribing this conversation, I try to learn from Pam: What did she do to make it work? There are concrete things: clearly and emphatically restating children's ideas; coaching children to look at and even open their hands to one another to help with listening; asking just the right mix of open-ended and clarifying questions. But there is something less tangible grounding all those specifics, a quality of "holding the space" that is familiar to me from places in my teaching life where I have confidence in both the "how" and "why" of what I am doing with children. Pam truly KNOWS what she is doing. She is clear about what she wants for the children—engagement, divergent thinking, critical analysis, listening to one another—and she is certain that spending time in this way will lead to those outcomes. She models patience and focus; she exudes an unshakable confidence in the value of each contribution, and an equally unshakable belief that the conversation will progress toward clarity. Her confidence is so abundant that she has enough to loan every other person in the room, including me; her energy creates a lively sense of curiosity, and her presence a sense of ease.

I had asked to see this, and as it unfolds, I am dazzled and humbled. I am a slow and deliberate learner of new skills, and I am well aware that I will not be able to replicate this kind of experience in a quick turn-around of skill development. But I feel my choices expand; I've got some signposts to follow, and a challenge to rise to.

And—in the short term—we have something interesting to think about with the children, a new addition to our Bad Guy lexicon: Protectors!

Protectors present a concrete and entirely non-violent solution to the problem of stopping badness. Now there is a legitimate alternative to banishing or killing the bad guy, and it's something we can MAKE. The icons Pam presents are familiar—they are, after all, bad guys—but they are also novel: bad guys co-opted by people and placed on buildings to create protection. Those gargoyles and lions and Jizo and totems really are, as Pam points out, a bit like our Library Bad Guy, but they are also different and mysterious enough to make the children think in a new way.

They represent a fascinating intersection of the two compelling ideas at the very heart of our Bad Guy Research: Badness and Protection. And, as I assume Pam suspected when she chose them, they appeal to the children's growing capacity to use bad guy imagery for their own purposes, including their mission to "Stop the Badness."

Pam, Sarah, and I talk about this conversation right after it happens. So far in the Bad Guy Research, we've done a lot of drawing, storytelling, acting, and pretending. But we have been watching for opportunities to expand the research into other expressive languages, and to try other avenues for thinking together in small groups. So we decide that Sarah will pursue the idea of building clay Protectors for the Children First playground.

Over the next few weeks, Sarah works with small groups on designing the Protectors. Each group decides, after considerable debate, what kind of creatures they'll build—dragons, owls and bears—and then sets to work on shaping and assembling the clay.

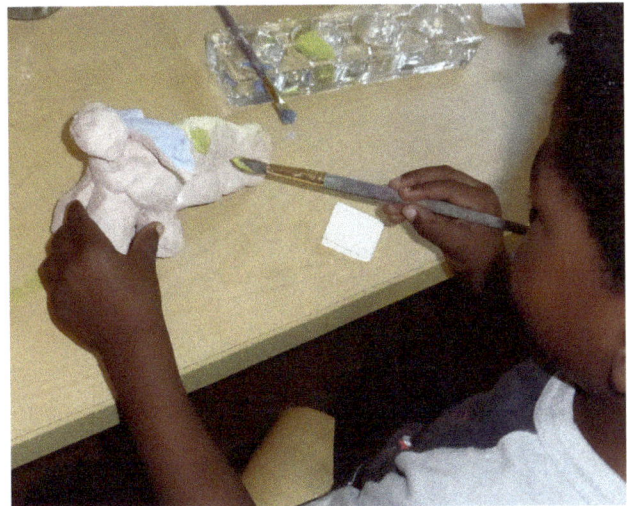

The protectors are sent to the kiln for firing, come back for glazing, and then go away again for their second firing. The sculptures are finished just a few days before Graduation. As it turns out, half of the children feel strongly that they need to take their Protectors home—not surprising when we remember Elisabeth saying earnestly to Pam, "I need to have one at my house." The other half will stay at school to protect the playground.

A Parent Survey about Protectors

For the older children, Parent Surveys are a staple of Children First curriculum. To conduct a survey, we decide on a question we want to ask family members—parents and sometimes siblings, too—and then choose which families each of us will be in charge of asking. The only rule is that you have to ask families that are not your own.

Already this year, we have asked every parent their age; their favorite color; and their favorite "sign of spring." We've asked them to tell us what they liked to play when they were kids, and how they like to play now. We've asked what name they would give their skin color; we've asked whether they cry, and how they stop crying; whether they've ever made a mistake, and if so, how they fixed it; what scares them and what helps them feel better when they're scared. We see surveys as useful practice with social skills and spoken language, requiring kids to approach adults with polite assertiveness: "Coby, do you have time for an interview?" But mostly we value surveys because they are one more strand in the web of "caring conspiracy" that connects each Children Firster to all the adults in the community.

So, as the Clay Protector work unfolds, it's not surprising that the kids eventually say, "Let's do a survey!" It's a conversation about the ways that mama birds hide and protect their eggs that leads us to the Big Question: If animal parents protect baby animals, do human parents protect baby humans?

Donna: Are our parents protectors?
Many: NO!
Miles: I think we should do an interview.
Elisabeth: Survey!
Donna: What would the question be?
Parker: What do you think—do you think a grown-up is a protector of a kid?
Donna: Wow. And then if they said "Yes" would you want to ask them how grownups protect kids?
Parker: Yeah.
Donna: OK, I think that's interesting.... And it sounds like y'all already have an opinion. Anybody think your parents are your protectors?
Elisabeth: Yeah.
Many: No.
Donna: Elisabeth, how do they protect you?
Elisabeth: Hmmm.... I don't know.

I'm intrigued to hear so many kids say that parents aren't their protectors. I wonder if it has to do with the usual push and pull older preschoolers often feel between independence and dependence, or if there is something especially provoking about this question when we ask it through the lens of Bad Guy Research. I'm curious to learn more about the children's thinking. So I create a chart with a list of parent names and put our question at the top: "Do you think parents are protectors for kids?" The children add their signs to the chart to indicate which parents they will ask.

I'm happy about this development.

The children's excitement tells me that this survey idea sparks their intellectual curiosity and speaks to their emotional disquiet about danger in the world.

And a survey will fold parents into our work in a simple but genuinely important way. They have been on the periphery of our Bad Guy Research, reading about it in portfolios and on display boards, but now they will be PART of that research. We know that what we do at school always has more reach and depth when it includes families. And because the question of protection and safety cuts so close to children's hearts, it seems especially important to give the people closest to them a chance to think about that question alongside us.

As the results come in over the next few weeks, one parent after another says "Yes, we are protectors for children!" In lunchtime conversations, I notice that the parents' responses spur shared commiseration about real-life worries, and reveal some interesting ambivalence in the children's dependence on adult protection. For instance:

Donna:	Do y'all feel like you need your parents to protect you?
Elisabeth:	I need them! I need them!
Lia:	I need them! Just in case a monster! Just in case a monster comes!
Parker:	Monsters are not real!
Lia:	Well, a pirate may come over to my land.
Parker:	No, pirates live all the way near Africa.
Lia:	Or a robber may come here.
Sam:	Robbers only used to be real, but now they're not.
Miles:	They're still real.... They're in China.

Note that Miles is, as he says, "half Chinese"—so this idea does not create quite the distance between him and the robbers that you might suppose.

Donna:	Robbers are only in China?	Donna:	You think everyone is protectors for everybody? Not just parents, but also kids?
Parker:	No, they're anywhere.		
Parker:	Pirates don't even come here.		
Miles:	Robbers are real.	Lia:	Kids are protectors for babies.
Parker:	Yeah, and a pirate is a type of robber. But pirates live all the way to Africa.	Donna:	Do you have to protect something younger than you, Lia?
Sam:	Pirates only steal treasure.	Lia:	Yes.
Miles:	Or money.	Donna:	Can you be a protector for something that's older than you?
Sam:	If they find it.		
Lia:	I wish I had seen a nice pirate.	Many:	No.
Elisabeth:	I always worry about pirates.	Elisabeth:	I'm a protector of my stuffed animals.

> I appreciate the way the children are grappling out loud with their worries about REAL badness, and finding support in doing it together.

On another day, as we count the growing number of "yeses" on the chart, the kids notice that I didn't give the reason for my own "yes" yet...

Parker: You can tell why.
Donna: Because parents are human animals, and animals are made to take care of their young.
Elisabeth: Everyone should take care of anyone else.

Lia: I'm a protector of my baby brother.
Parker: Because I think that kids can learn just by seeing, by just seeing older kids that are doing right things like for example, like, like a little kid like a three-year-old that likes to cry, like seeing an older kid that's like 8, not crying, will help them learn.
Donna: Oh, so parents don't have to teach kids everything, because kids can learn from older kids who are role models?
Parker: Uh huh.
Donna: Do you think that happens at Children First with older kids and younger kids?
Parker: Yeah.

Here the children give us concrete examples of the way that they themselves are powerful protectors. Now I understand more about their occasional insistence that parents are NOT protectors, despite their very own parents' insistence that they are.

The children want parent protection, but they do not want that protection to diminish their own value and competence.

Another day, we read that Sam's dad believes parents are protectors because they make food for their children.

Lia:	And I know another thing, cause kids don't know how to cook.
Sam:	And then they won't grow up.
Donna:	Because you need food to grow?
Sam:	Yeah.
Parker:	And also sometimes they can't reach the stuff off the top of the refrigerator that they need to feed the dog or cat.
Miles:	And I would say yes because the grown-ups love their kids.
Donna:	So Miles you think love is part of protecting, huh? That's a powerful idea.

At lunch on the very last day of school, I place the completed survey on the table, and read the last few answers.

Donna:	So what do you think—are parents protectors for kids?
Parker:	Yes, Yes, Yes—all yes.
Donna:	It seems clear that all of your parents are going to do their best to protect y'all.

As the children study this "hard evidence" of their parents' collective commitment to keep them safe, there is a palpable feeling of ease and contentment around the table. It's reassuring and empowering to be told in such a definitive way that your grown-ups intend to take care of you. When Parker and Alena insist on the last word—"I'm a protector for myself!" and "I can protect my parents!"—I hear children who feel secure and strong. Indeed, Parker *is* more able to protect herself when she knows her parents have her back; and Alena *will* find ways to contribute to her parents' sense of safety and well-being in the world, because they have contributed to hers. We are, truly, protectors for each other in our shared quest to "Stop the Badness."

Do you think Parents are Protectors for Kids?

Parent...	who asks?	Yes or No?	Why?
Adrienne		**Yes** No	b/c
Rashad		**Yes** No	that's what dad intended
Al	LIA	**Yes** No	b/c parents love their kids, you try to protect the love — parents are
Jessica	LIA	Yes No	b/c parents have lots of experience + have learned from that — when Avery had a bg d bum about bean I walked him back to his room so he wouldn't feel sad
Summer		**Yes** No	
Stephen		**Yes** No	b/c kids need help or guidance making decisions + know then feel ok
Elizabeth		**Yes** No	b/c I think that's my #1 job to keep my kid safe
Fabian		**Yes** No	when you're young you don't have as much experience about what is dangerous like fire is hot —
Craig		**Yes** No	The most important b/c they're the closest to them until they get old enough to take care of themselves
Nikki		**Yes** No	parents because we're adults we know what's safe + unsafe
Donna		**Yes** No	b/c parents are human animals animals are made to take care their young
Sarah		**Yes** No	the grown ups are bigger

I created this chart to help the older kids organize their survey. They drew the child's sign to the left of each parent pair, and then added their own name or sign beside the parents they would take charge of asking. So you see Aiden's "bee" beside his parents Adrienne and Rashad, and Elisabeth's "wrench" tells us she will be the one who approaches them with this question.

PROTECTION FROM BADNESS

CHAPTER 7

Finding Power in Shared Story Making

Soon after we begin work on the Clay Protectors, an incidental encounter lands me squarely at the intersection of those two competing teacher commitments: my aspiration to be a researcher working alongside the children, and my responsibility to be a caregiver assuring children that they're safe. Driving my van on one of our weekly outings to the Eno River, I listen as the five kids in the backseat trade opinions about some deer statues they see in a yard: Are they alive? If not, what ARE they? Concrete? Wood? Or maybe clay! Here, I inject a casual comment: "This talk about clay makes me think of the clay protectors y'all are going to build." And then Miles asks a question in a somber tone that is anything but casual: "But will it even work?" His poignant query releases a flood of emotion, as one kid after the other echoes the question "Will it work?" or answers with sighs of resignation, "Yeah, it won't work." Are they worried that clay is not a good material for building protectors? Or do they mean that clay protectors will not really keep them safe? Before I can ask, the kids shift their attention to the river morning ahead, and I let the moment pass.

Later, however, I share the conversation with Sarah, and write to Pam about it, too:

> This tender little exchange reminds me that when the kids are building the protectors with Sarah, she will want to be alert to REAL anxiety about whether the protectors will be up for the job.

My hunch is that the kids may need us to acknowledge that the protectors they are making are about pretend bad guys—and yes, that is serious "research business"—but that if there was any protection needed from real bad guys around here, the grown-ups will have their backs.

When I write these words, I have no clue that we are about to step into a whole new arena of Bad Guy Battling, a place where brave and ingenious Kid Protectors will harness the power of teamwork and technology to thoroughly dispatch and defeat badness in its most intimidating forms. The children are about to show us that, at least in their stories, they can take care of themselves.

Fumbling to Find a Way Forward

The Bad Guy Battling begins with a morning of disappointing small group conversations. As Sarah launches her work on building the clay protectors, I decide that I will follow up on an idea we've heard in several recent descriptions of badness: "Bad guys are angry." I am always curious about the intersection between bad guy badness and the real life "badness" that the children experience themselves. I wonder what they make of anger: where it comes from, how it feels in their bodies, where it goes. And I'm especially curious about whether they consider anger a bad thing in and of itself, or whether they make the same distinction I do: feeling angry is fine, but doing hurtful things out of anger is not. I have an agenda here; I want kids to take responsibility for what they *do*, but I never want them to deny or denigrate what they *feel*. So, while I'm genuinely curious about the children's thinking, I also want to suss out whether any of them "need" my intervention and support to come into healthy relationship with the emotion of anger. With these mixed motives humming in the back of my mind, I bring small groups into the library and invite them to draw and talk about anger.

I begin the meeting by reading back some of their own words about "angry bad guys." And then I say, "I want to know more about your ideas. Maybe draw a bad guy, and show me the anger inside a bad guy."

The conversations that follow feel flat and prickly from beginning to end. In some groups, the energy is polite, but the answers feel rote and forced. But my meeting with Avery, Miles, Parker and Lia is especially unpleasant. There's a lot of "I don't know" that sounds like "I don't care." Avery is busy mimicking Miles; the conversation degenerates into slapstick as kids add silly details to their drawings

and laugh together over words like "nipple" and "belly button"—words they enjoy calling "disgusting" and "funny as a pig." The kids respond to my re-direction and limit-setting with suspicion and even resentment as they get loud and unruly. When I ask, "How do people calm down when they get angry?" they say, "By pushing other people and hitting their eyeballs." Miles wrinkles his paper, and Avery uses his fine-point marker to draw on his face. All in all, I leave these conversations feeling more like a boss than a facilitator, an "outsider" who is doing something *to* the children, not someone researching *with* them. I feel embarrassed about the whole fiasco, but I also know that, if I want to learn, this is exactly the moment when I should turn to Sarah and Pam—my trusted co-teacher and pedagogical guide—for honest feedback and guidance. So, I send Pam and Sarah the transcriptions of the small group conversations and ask if we can look at them together.

Sarah and I talk with Pam by phone the next day. Despite my discomfort, it's a satisfying conversation. First of all, there is something freeing about inviting my colleagues to look squarely at my "bad work." I do *feel* shame, but I choose to behave as though I genuinely believe in my right to learn from mistakes. In the end, Pam doesn't have a lot to say about what I did wrong. She acknowledges that I have been a little stubborn about sticking with a question that didn't connect with the children's intentions, but she clearly thinks that some awkward conversations and rejected provocations are just part of the process. As a pedagogical companion, what interests her more is finding a place in the conversation where kids DID come alive in their thinking.

And maybe she's found it. She brings us back to what I consider the "worst" meeting—the one where Avery, Miles, Lia and Parker got so loud and silly. Pam is interested in the "globes" that the older kids drew around their bad guys. This line of thinking began when the children dressed their angry bad guys in "goggles" and "stinky old clothes" because "they like dirty clothes." We re-read that part of the conversation together.

Then Miles draws an enclosure around his bad guy...

Miles:	And they want to be in a globe so he's in a globe.
Parker:	A globe around him, like a big globe. A live globe with a live person in it, a live bad guy.
Donna:	Can he get out of there, Miles, or is it like a trap?
Miles:	It's a trap.
Donna:	A trap is like a protection against bad guys, I guess.
Elisabeth:	He's trapped all right.

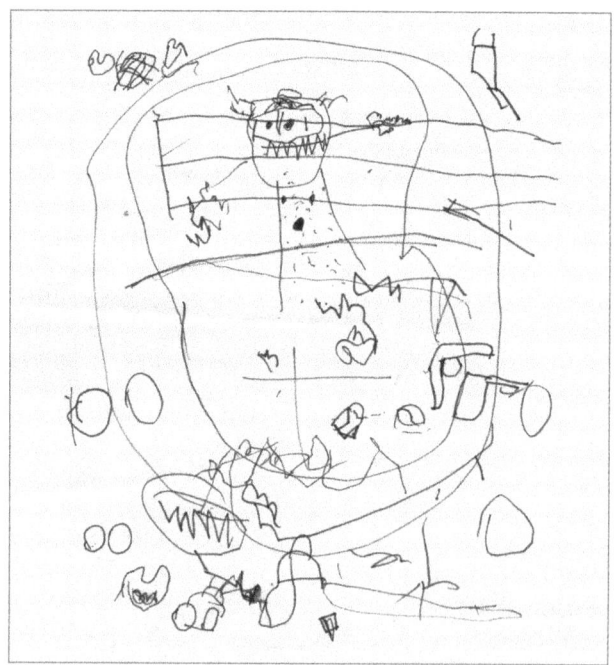

Miles draws the bad guy trapped in a globe and covered with a big E because "he doesn't like E's."

So, Pam says, maybe you want to find out more about those globes.

I'm relieved that these conversations may not be a complete loss. I find myself spinning a grand vision of children building giant Bad Guy Globes together. I e-mail Pam and Sarah about my idea, describing how I'll provision with poster board and materials from the creation station, and make copies of the Library Bad Guy that the children can put inside the globes they build.

Pam issues her usual reminder—slow down, listen—and her usual reassurance that what's important will never get lost. And Sarah points out that the kids should probably take the lead on which bad guy, if any, will be part of the work. I take a deep breath, take a day off from structured conversation to watch children play, and then propose another plan:

I'll invite a group of four or five children to meet, including some who drew the globe last time, and at least one who wasn't here for that, and I'll share my interest in the idea of globes around bad guys. And I'll bring pens and paper; if an idea for "building a globe" emerges, we will take time to think carefully about design and materials before launching into the actual work.

Not a Globe, but a Book

So, a full week after the awkward anger conversations, I'm back in the library with five kids: three of the four who were part of the original globe conversation (Lia is absent today), along with Elisabeth and Sam. Just as we're about to begin, Alena knocks insistently on the library door, and we invite her to join us, too.

Donna: Last week some kids came into the library—when Sam was sick—to do some bad guy research and this really interesting idea came up. Sam hasn't heard about this idea so I thought he might want to know more about it, and I do, too.

I hand out a page where I've collected all the drawings that Parker, Avery, Lia and Miles made depicting Bad Guys in Globes.

Donna: I was studying these drawings you did and I was curious to hear more about these things you drew around the bad guys. Do you remember the word you used for them?

PURSUING BAD GUYS

Parker: Traps.
Miles: No, I made them be globes.
Sam: What are globes?
Parker: They can't walk around the earth; it's like a trap for the bad guys.

Parker takes a snow globe from a nearby table and holds it up for our consideration…

Donna: Oh, so you were thinking the bad guy was inside a globe like this.

Avery: Yeah.
Donna: What do you put inside the globes?
Parker: Yucky things that they don't like.
Sam: I think poison. Poison falling down, like when you shake it.

Notice how quickly Sam "catches on" to this idea he's just heard for the first time.

Donna: How does the bad guy get in the globe?

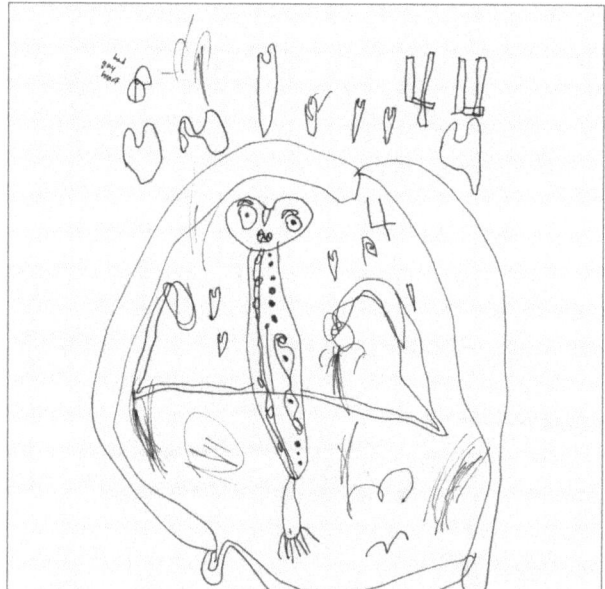

ABOVE LEFT: *Lia draws the bad guy trapped in a rainbow globe "with hearts to annoy him."* **ABOVE RIGHT:** *Avery draws the bad guy with his "disgusting shooter" and then adds hearts "because he doesn't like hearts."* **OPPOSITE PAGE:** *Parker shows the bad guy trapped in a globe with "good guy toys he doesn't like" and wearing shabby old clothes with holes.*

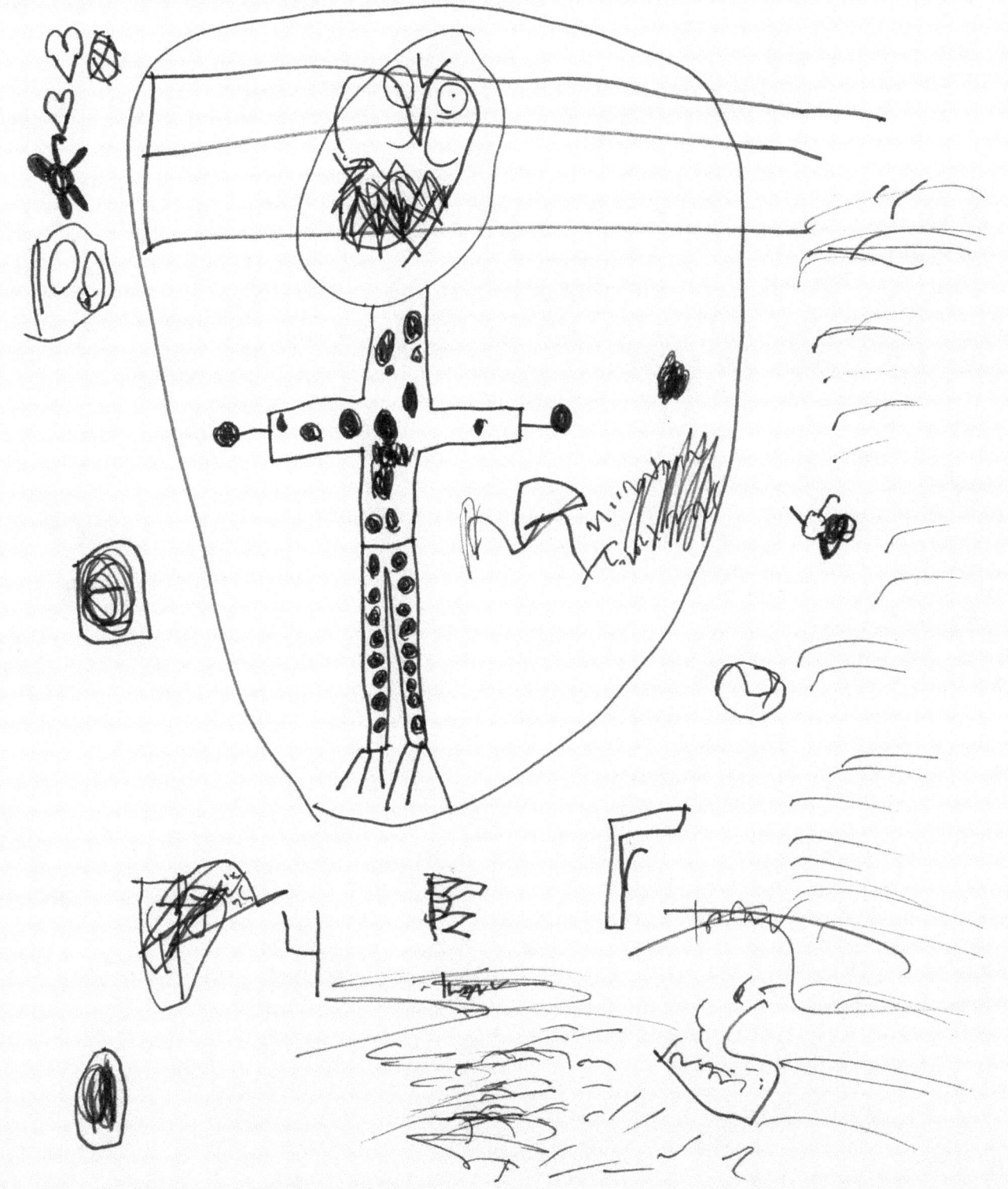

Parker:	They trap him. It's too strong, that he can't open it up.
Donna:	You mean, they open it and he goes in?
Parker:	Uh huh, but he can't open it once he's in.
Donna:	They close it?
Parker:	Yeah.
Donna:	Who is 'they'? Who is doing the trapping?
Parker:	The regular people.
Donna:	Good guys?
Parker:	Uh huh.
Elisabeth:	Or Good Girls.
Miles:	Maybe we could do a story of these?

I am genuinely surprised (and also delighted) by this idea.

Donna:	Do you want to do one now?

Many: Sure.
Donna: Would it be like people each told their own story, or one all together?
Many: Everybody.

I'm almost certain that this moment would not have happened before the Bad Guy Research. For one thing, I probably would not have invited the group to do one story all together. And even if I had, I think some of the kids would have insisted on doing their own story, the usual way. Their vision of themselves as collaborators who create together, as a group, has really grown.

Donna: How's it going to start?
Parker: OK, who's going to start anyway?

And there's Parker, organizing the process... the kids sort out a plan: they'll take turns, clockwise around the table. And I decide that, even though I'm recording, I'll also write the story dictation-style: this is the storytelling rhythm the kids know well, and it allows me to reflect back what I'm hearing and creates little pauses for thinking between parts of the story. As we proceed, there are meanderings and negotiations, side tours and leaps of collective imagination.

Here's the story as I read it back to the children after a solid half-hour of co-construction:

Once upon a time, there was the globe. And then some good people found it. And then a bad guy came and the nice people trapped the bad guy in the globe. And then they put the whole globe thing with the bad guy inside into jail. And then they put bars on him, around the globe AND inside the globe, and the bars trapped the bad guy and held his whole body really tight. And then the good guys made a hole and poured poison into the globe. And then the good people un-trapped the jail and then the jail was gone. And then mean people trapped the bad guy in the globe and put him in another place really far away, all the way in outer space where the gas planets are that you don't live on, that are made out of gas. The bad guy was NOT living on earth. And then some mean people went to the globe and threw sweet toys and sweet hearts into the globe, because that's what the bad guy does NOT like. And then the globe fell off the planet. And then the globe went back to outer space into the other planets, and landed on a star. And then the bad guy died.

Alena: (quietly, and with a sly smile) And then another bad guy comes.

We all ignore Alena's "conclusion busting" suggestion for now.

Donna: He lands on a star and then he dies?
Many: Yeah!
Miles: And that's the end.

Miles sounds relieved, almost exhausted. This bad guy has been on quite a journey, and so have we.

Donna: Miles, you're ready for it to be over.
Miles: Yeah.

My instinct is that Miles is not alone in this feeling. There is a palpable sense of relief around the table at having so thoroughly disposed of this bad guy. But I can't leave Alena's idea unheard; I want the group to be a safe place for every voice, especially the voice of the youngest and quietest member.

Donna: Alena just did something really interesting though. In a big book, what we just did would be like the end of a chapter, and in the next chapter, it might be like what Alena just said—
Alena: And then more bad guys come.
Donna: We don't have to write that story today. But that's how it is in real books a lot. You think everything is fixed and OK, and the chapter is over, and then… uh oh—it's not over yet. Chapter 2….Should I just write that, and then we could write it another day?

There is a pause, satisfied, and I am ready to get back to the idea I had in mind all along—the possibility of building a globe…

Donna: So, there was this one other idea I was thinking about…

But before I can (somewhat foolishly) forge ahead with my pre-conceived idea…

Parker: It's like a book.
Donna: It IS like a book.

And then suddenly it's like a firecracker has gone off. There is pandemonium around the table.

LET'S MAKE A BOOK! LET'S MAKE A BOOK!

After some literal screaming and yelling comes a flood of thoughts…

Sam:	But what's it gonna be called?
Miles:	We can use staples to staple it together.
Donna:	What's the first chapter called?
Sam:	The Globe!
Many:	Yeah.
Avery:	The title is...
Miles:	The book.
Someone:	Bad Guys.
Avery:	The title is "Bad Guys."

I am flabbergasted, and exhilarated! Not a globe, but a book! Sign me up!

Donna:	Oh my gosh. So it looks like I have a job. I'll take all these notes and go to my computer and make them into tidy pages for the first chapter of the story. We'll come back on Monday so you can illustrate the pages, like a real picture book. And then we'll be ready to write Chapter 2.
Sam:	But how much chapters is there?
Miles:	How about like 10?
Elisabeth:	How about 3?
Sam:	10?
Donna:	We can see what happens when we start telling it. We may feel like "That should be the end" or "There's another idea and it's so fantastic we need Chapter 5 or whatever."

We end the meeting in a buoyant and happy mood—me perhaps most of all. I have my next mission in the Bad Guy Research! And it really truly came from the kids! Hurrah! I had come prepared to "make something"—work that would be way out of my comfort zone—and here come the kids, taking us back to storytelling, my favorite place to be. And I know that I did not lead them there; I had been especially vigilant about listening, waiting and following.

> Once we began the story,
> I was delighted by the way
> the children came to a
> joyful creative consensus,
> undaunted by the focus,
> discussion, and compromise
> the process demanded.

In last week's conversation, I was dragging a raft against the current; today, we are riding a wave together.

We meet again on Monday. I explain that I've listened to the recording of our first conversation and written the story down, and I offer to read it aloud "to make sure I got it right." Revisiting the story together is both exciting—"Wow! We really wrote that!"—and businesslike, since the children are accustomed to having their stories read back for editing. Overall, they are still palpably enthralled with Chapter 1, suggesting just a few small changes here and there.

Donna: Does it feel complete?

All: Yes.

Parker: That's Chapter 1.

And with that, we turn our attention to how the chapter will be illustrated. Ideas are proposed, considered, modified, and countered, until Alena suggests a mathematically elegant plan to which everyone agrees. We'll have three chapters in the book. One person will illustrate Chapter 1, a job which Parker began lobbying for the moment she sat down.

FINDING POWER IN SHARED STORY MAKING

The plan for illustrating each chapter, using the children's signs—Parker's pants; Sam's birdhouse and Avery's lunchbox; Alena's watermelon, Elisabeth's wrench and Miles' police car.

Two children—Sam and Avery—will illustrate Chapter Two. And the remaining children—Miles, Alena and Elisabeth—will illustrate Chapter 3. Parker puts the illustrator commitments into chart form, making it official. With that plan settled, everyone settles in to "sketch our ideas for Parker" so she will know what the group as a whole thinks Chapter 1 should look like. Around the table, each of the kids creates their own images of the story, discussing and debating details as they draw. When Parker makes the final illustrations, she will incorporate her friends' ways of imagining the gas planets, the sweet toys and hearts, the bars and chains on the globe, and the Bad Guy himself.

Alena's sketch of the bad guy with big teeth and a nose like a watermelon.

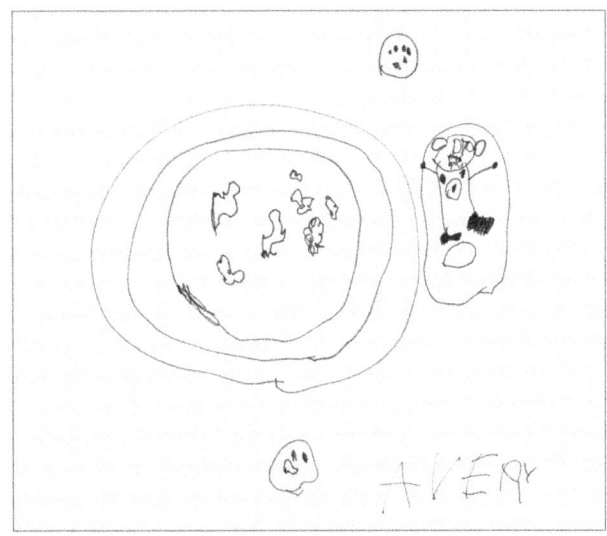

Avery's sketch of the bad guy on the bouncy gas planet with his hair "burned off" and earth far away.

FINDING POWER IN SHARED STORY MAKING

Parker's final illustrations for Chapter One, incorporating details from all her friends' sketches: the bad guy inside the globe inside the jail; the bad guy inside the globe, standing on the gas planet, with the sweet things he dislikes inside the globe with him; and the bad guy falling off the gas planet and onto a star, where his hair gets burned off.

From Clarity to Confusion

I send Chapter 1 to Pam, excited to hear her response. The kids are so pleased with their work, and have been excited to share it with their families and to act the story at meeting for the whole group. As for me, I am giddy with excitement about the whole process: the organic emergence of the story, the engaged and animated editing process, and the ingenious solution to the problem of who and how to illustrate each chapter. There has been such a gorgeous flow to this work: heart and ease, humor and seriousness, individual opinion and collectivity of intention, all in a beautiful balance. Pam sees this, too, and offers some specific encouragement about my facilitation: "I really like how you got out of the children's way in this conversation, while supporting, clarifying, and challenging as warranted."

I'm eager for more, and Chapter 2 awaits. But I'm also nervous that I will do something to break the spell. I feel a little like Cinderella at the Reggio Ball, waiting for the chime of the clock that will catapult me back to my usual cinders. I have never believed I would be THAT teacher, the one co-constructing amazing projects with her kids.

Also, I've heard all the criticism about the superficial quasi-projects happening out in "imitation Reggio world." I would rather sidestep co-constructed research altogether than teach with only the trappings and not the substance of authentic Reggio-inspired work. But it seems I'm really here, hanging out with kids on their way to making a high quality piece of creative work, work coming straight from their collective emotional and intellectual center.

I desperately want the writing of additional chapters, however many that proves to be, to happen with the same authentic energy and momentum that created the first one. But because the process is unfolding by trial and error, I worry that I will spoil the magic with some ill-timed, self-centered or clumsy move. Pam and Sarah don't seem particularly worried, which is, in its way, reassuring. But in fact, the first conversation about Chapter 2 does not go well at all.

Avery declines to join—perhaps a bad omen—so I gather the other five and present Chapter 1, which I've put into a binder with Parker's illustrations:

Donna: Here's the Bad Guy chapter book, with a cover Sam drew. I thought I'd begin by reading this, and then I'll add the words Alena wanted to add when we finished the story...

I read the chapter, showing Parker's illustrations.

Donna: The End. And that's when Alena said, "And then the bad guy came back."
Alena: It could be a girl.
Parker: It's not.
Donna: Is Chapter 2 going to be that this bad guy comes back, or a totally different bad guy?
Alena: A totally different bad guy.
Elisabeth: Totally different.
Many: Different.
Donna: So that Chapter 1 bad guy really will be dead forever, and Chapter 2 will be a new bad guy?
Parker: I don't want it to be a girl.
Elisabeth: Yeah. No girl.

Beginning with this stubborn disagreement about Bad Guy gender—a debate that had already been brewing between these girls—the conversation stumbles discordantly toward a catalogue of possible bad guy characters, with no real momentum toward agreement and a disappointing absence of excitement about any of the possibilities. We end the meeting without anything decided, and I'm queasy; maybe I have already broken the spell of Chapter 1!

Disappointed, I send the transcription, along with my commentary, to Pam. I preface the e-mail with this note:

> And here is a pretty miserable little effort to begin exploring Chapter 2. You'll see that I've included a fair amount of self-reflection in my transcription of the conversation. At least I'm starting to notice all the ways I go too fast; miss important moments; and give too many either/or questions to the kids, questions that lock them in to my presuppositions. It's painful to realize these things, but I guess that's the way it goes, because, as we say around here, "I'm still learning."
>
> ANYWAY...After hanging out with all this documentation today, my current thought is to hand the group a one-page collection of the bad guys they drew today, and to ask something like, "When I looked at all these bad guys you drew together, I wondered if they might be a team."

My reasoning for this somewhat leading question is that I get the feeling that simply combining their drawings physically will be a gesture of "together" that I think may be soothing and reassuring after all the disagreement today, and that bringing the important word "team" to the table as a possibility may also be helpful. One thing I wonder is whether they will ever come up with a story plan about a good guy team to dispatch the bad guys, something that I also think might feel really good and integrating to them, but which I will not suggest myself.

Pam gets back to me quickly, offering lots of encouragement and one recommendation:

> I like the idea of bringing all the Chapter 2 drawings back to the group. But maybe hold off on leading the children toward thinking about a team of bad guys. It's good to keep that possibility in the back of your mind in case you need it. But if you show the children the drawings and they can SEE the divergence of opinion about this chapter (and, if necessary, you articulate the problem, just as it is, without "choices"), they may come up with a completely different strategy. Or that very strategy. Does that make sense?

Reassured, I respond...

> I think I understand your suggestion about the conversation. I'll have the scanned drawings put together on one page for their consideration. I'll give them out. I'll say something like, "These are the drawings y'all did about ideas for Chapter 2. There were a lot of different opinions." And then wait and listen...

And the next day, that's what I do.

A Roller Coaster of a Conversation

Late in the morning, I bring the five children who drew together last time, along with Avery, into an informal gathering on the floor of the block area. I sense that it might help to meet somewhere other than the library, where our last conversation ground to such an unproductive halt. In any case, I have done my best to mentally prepare so that I can be patient, open, and relaxed about the outcome of the conversation.

Donna: I brought something for you to look at.

I hand out the pages with the scanned drawings of bad guys the children drew during our last conversation.

Right away, there is a lot of conversation along the lines of "This one's mine" and identifying what each person drew.

Donna: A lot of different opinions.
Avery: I really like Miles'. I really like the Storm Trooper.

More "This is mine" all around, repeated many times.

Miles: What if we said, "All of the ones on the back are mine." Like, "These are ALL mine."

Many repeat this idea.

Sam: These are all everybody's!

This is seen as a joke, and more silliness ensues.

Miles' Storm Trooper.

FINDING POWER IN SHARED STORY MAKING

Sam's Robber.

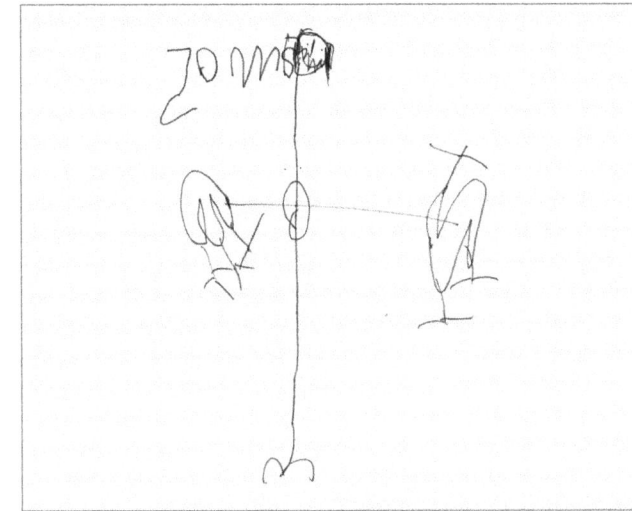

Elisabeth's Zombie.

Parker's Zombie.

Alena's Darth Vader.

I am waiting and listening and watching. The talk gets progressively sillier and rowdier. Finally I speak, but slowly and quietly.

Donna: So, Children Firsters, what I'm seeing right now is some goofing, which is fun, but I'm not sure it's going to help us with Chapter 2.

Momentary pause, then back to goofing. Without rancor, I offer an out, one I fully expect the children to take.

Donna: So, if we're not going to talk about Chapter 2, we could just go ahead and play.
Many: Noooo.

They seem sincere. But in fact, as we continue, so does the goofing. I name what is happening.

Donna: So, the silly playing is still happening and nobody is talking about Chapter 2.

And then Sam makes a try at turning us to the story.

Sam: I wonder what's gonna happen.
Avery: I don't know.
Parker: Me, too.

Stuck again, the group tips back toward goofing... but then Avery speaks quietly—so quietly that I'm the only one who seems to hear him. I get the other children's attention and ask him to repeat what he said.

Avery: These are the new people and a new friend is coming to school. To THIS school.
Parker: Who is it?
Avery: Don't know who it is.
Miles: The monsters?
Avery: No, new people.
Donna: Avery, did you mean a bad guy is coming to school, or a person who's not a bad guy?
Avery: A person who is not a bad guy.

Skeptical sounds from the older children...

Sam: What are you talking about?

Donna: Tell us more about your idea, Avery. You were just saying your idea about a new person coming to the school…

Avery: That a new person like… a new person I don't know, but like a new person that's coming here, but you haven't met—like with the grown-ups, you haven't met in the library yet.

Now I understand exactly what Avery's talking about: he's describing an Admissions Visit, when I meet in the library with prospective parents, and the child—the potential "new person"—plays in the classroom. We've been hosting a lot of these visits lately.

Donna: So it's like a visiting kid?
Elisabeth: Ohhhhh.
Donna: Like, "Once upon a time, at Children First, there was a visitor kid at school."
Elisabeth: I got it.
Miles: I got it.
Sam: I don't got it.
Donna: Well, we've had a lot of kids visiting—when I'm in the library meeting with the parents, and the kid is playing at Children First. What if the story started with a visiting kid?
Sam: Oh, now I get this.
Donna: So, what if the story started at Children First with a visiting kid? Avery had us starting at Children First with a visitor coming… Is the visiting kid a bad guy, Avery?
Avery: No.
Donna: OK, it's a kid.
Parker: That's not a bad guy, I guess.

Notice Parker treating Avery's idea respectfully; she's leading a shift towards collective purposeful engagement in the conversation. And from there, the kids begin, just as they did in Chapter 1, to build the plot together, trading ideas, debating details, gaining momentum and, ultimately arriving at a breathtaking story about the power of a team to face down one truly terrifying embodiment of badness.

Avery: And then we win! And then we win!
Elisabeth: We win!

When I transcribe this roller coaster of a conversation, I'm amazed at the way it began with such extreme factionalism—each child promoting his or her own bad guy idea—and ended with a consensus to make a story about one all-inclusive Good Guy Team.

Here's the final version, after another lively session of collective editing, including a heated debate about the title, and another meeting to generate guide sketches for our Chapter Two illustrators, Sam and Avery.

Chapter 2: Invisible Goggles

Once upon a time on a weekend day, there is a little kid visiting Children First with his Mom and Dad. The Mom and Dad and kid are on the playground, and Donna and Sarah are inside, and are not watching the playground.

Suddenly, a huge monster, bigger than a hotel in New York, comes all the way from China into the woods to the south of Children First. He leaps over the fence and goes on the zipline and stomps onto the playground. The Mom and Dad and kid are really scared, and they say "Eeeek!" and "Oh no!" They start to move back to get away from the monster.

Avery shows the two visiting parents and their small child moving away from the giant monster, with Donna and Sarah far away inside the school. Notice that Avery uses a spiral—the "sign" for Children First as a school—to indicate that the building is the Children First classroom.

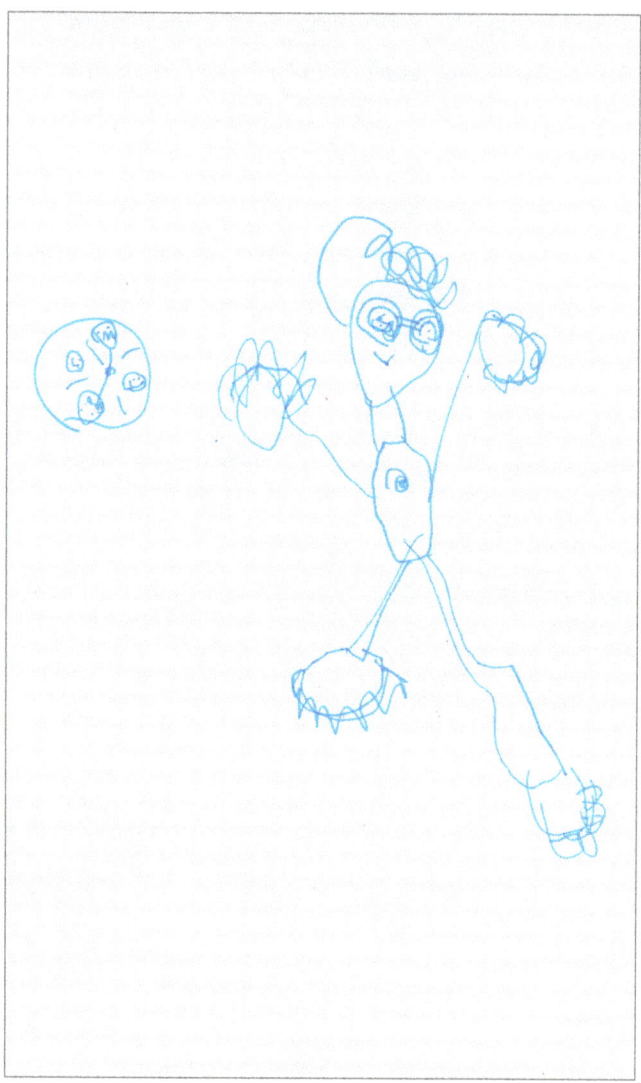

Meanwhile, all the Children First kids are at their houses. But they have special clocks with alarms that go off when there is a danger in the world. They hear the alarm and see the hand pointed to "Monster." Then they put on their magic goggles and turn them so they can see all the way to Children First. They see the monster!

They grab some snack in case they get hungry or bored, then use their goggles to turn themselves invisible, and hurry to Children First! They hide behind trees to spy on the monster. The monster cannot see them, and the grown-ups cannot see them, and the little kid cannot see them, but they can see each other because the whole team of Children Firsters has the same magic goggles, and even when they are being invisible, they can see each other's goggles.

When the monster gets to the mulch in front of the library, the Children Firsters come out of their hiding places, and tackle the monster.

ABOVE: *Sam draws a Children Firster as he notices his "clock pointing to monsters" and puts on his goggles. Again, note that Sam adds a spiral to the t-shirt to indicate that the person with the clock is a Children First kid.* **OPPOSITE PAGE:** *Starting with our playground map, which we've used in earlier conversations about where Bad Guys might live, Sam shows the monster looming over the library, and then adds 12 sets of goggles hiding out in strategic locations.*

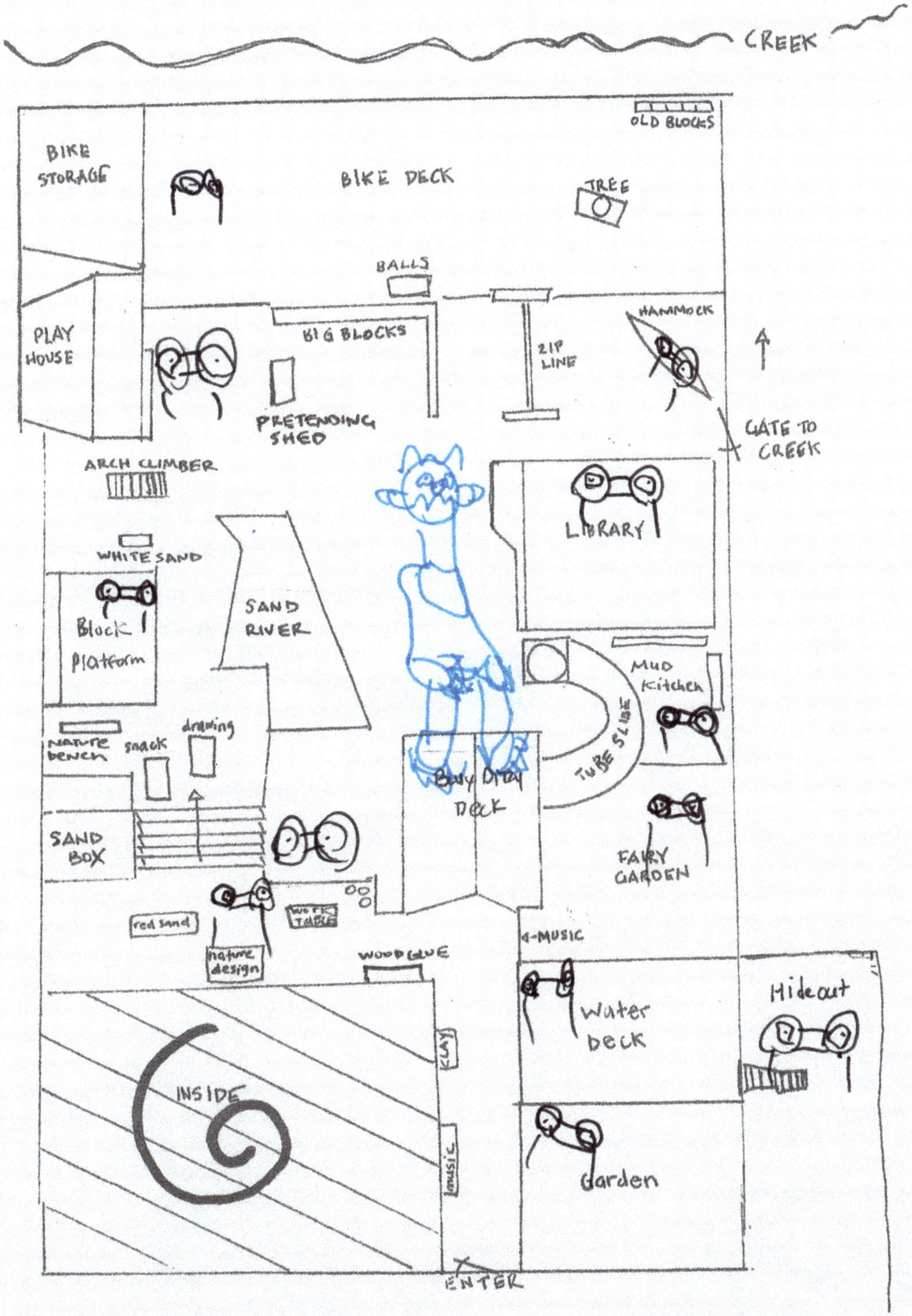
CREEK
OLD BLOCKS
BIKE STORAGE
BIKE DECK
TREE
BALLS
PLAY HOUSE
BIG BLOCKS
ZIP LINE
HAMMOCK
GATE TO CREEK
PRETENDING SHED
ARCH CLIMBER
LIBRARY
WHITE SAND
SAND RIVER
Block Platform
Mud Kitchen
TUBE SLIDE
nature bench
snack
drawing
Deck
SAND BOX
FAIRY GARDEN
red sand
WORK TABLE
nature design
WOOD GLUE
MUSIC
Water deck
Hideout
CLAY
INSIDE
music
Garden
ENTER

PURSUING BAD GUYS

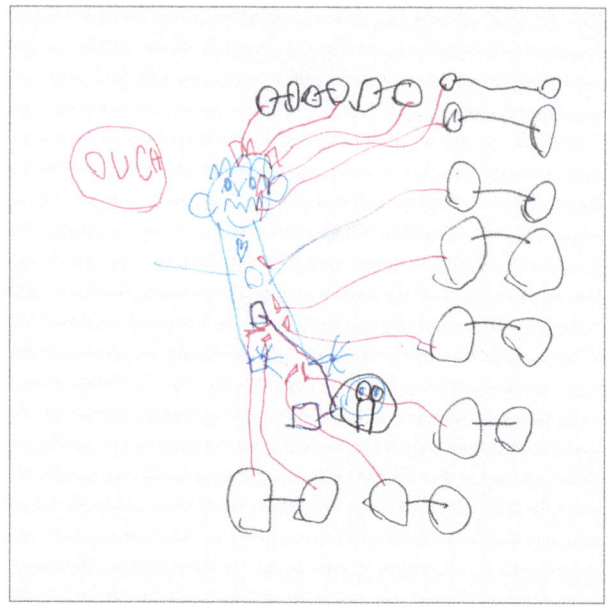

The monster yells "Ouchie! Ouchie!" Then the kids yell "Ouch!" and pretend they are hurt, but instead they twist away from the monster and jump up high and kick him in the belly.

That monster is so confused! He has NO IDEA what is happening, because he can't see what's hitting him and kicking him. He says "Ouch! Ouch! Ouch!"

The Children Firsters win the fight, because there are 12 on their team, and the monster is only one. When the monster is halfway dead, the kids drag him to the creek and throw him in the icky sticky mud. His tongue goes in the mud and he throws up and dies all the way.

The Children Firsters take off their goggles, and now the little kid and his parents know who saved them. They say, "Thank you!" and then they go home.

ABOVE LEFT: Avery shows the kids, with only their goggles visible, attacking the monster, who yells "Ouch!" The red lines trace the contact between the kids and the monster. **BOTTOM LEFT:** Sam shows the halfway dead monster sticking his tongue in the creek and then throwing up something green. **OPPOSITE PAGE:** With the monster dispatched, Sam can unveil the children's true identities—represented by the signs on their bodies—to the visitors they have saved. Adding a speech bubble, he lets his young friend Oliver voice the satisfaction of the battle—"That was fun!"—while the visiting parents say, "Thanks."

Avery shows Donna and Sarah coming out to thank the kids for their heroic effort—no arms needed for these by-standing teachers!

And Donna and Sarah look out the window and see the Children Firsters and say, "Thank you SO much for getting that monster away from our playground!" The End.

When I share the chapter with Pam, Sarah and Children First families, I also share my reflections about what happened.

When Avery, the oldest child in his family but the youngest in this group, first suggested the visitor, his tone had a quiet intensity that let me know his idea was heartfelt and important. After all, consider what he accomplishes with the choice to cast "a kid visitor" as the character under threat. The endangered character is enough like him to make the story thrilling, but enough different that he himself can feel safe. The character is younger, weaker, less knowledgeable—needing rescue by the competent older team—perhaps the victim is a stand-in for his little brother. It's brilliant. I'm so glad I managed to bring his idea forward for the group to really consider, and I'm thrilled that he persisted in the face of skepticism and interruptions. Pam always says that when an idea has power for kids, it will come back—and sure enough, this one did.

I love the way the kids found their way to "Team," such an important and fraught idea for them all year. Throughout the conversation, I felt their intensity around forming alliances and jockeying for position within those alliances. Notice that the victory over the monster was secured not only by the children's tricks, tools and well-honed "wrassling" power (Sam's word for "wrestling" and a word that has become super important to the group) but also by their numerical advantage, an advantage strengthened when they agreed to include not just the kids telling the story, but all 12 Children Firsters on one Good Guy Team. And what a cohesive Team they are, connected by their alarm clocks even at their individual houses.

I also love the way this story works with ideas of place. There is "China"—a place far away, but also connected to us through Miles, who strongly identifies as "half-Chinese." There is New York, a city Parker visits often—the home of skyscrapers that help us understand just how huge this monster really is. And there is the relationship of the land around the playground—outside the fence and down at the creek—with the fenced playground itself—an important invocation of inside/outside that speaks to safety and belonging. And of course, there is the new connection between home and school that is facilitated by the magical clocks.

Finally, it's interesting—and perhaps a bit genius—that the bad guy threat in the story is not actually represented by any of the individual drawings from the first fractured conversation. Instead, the children invented a whole new bad guy, in a form that has been consistently important in their storytelling: a huge monster. When Pam said, "They might come up with a whole new strategy," she was right!

As with Chapter 1, we meet again as a group to work on drawings that will guide Avery and Sam's final illustrations for the chapter. I admire the many careful and detailed drawings that the boys create, but it's Avery's simple illustration for the final page that really leaves me smiling.

"And Donna and Sarah look out the window and see the Children Firsters and say, 'Thank you SO much for getting that monster away from our playground!' The End."

At first, seeing these teachers, drawn with few features and no arms, I am a little frustrated with Avery; I think maybe he is getting tired and taking shortcuts. I ask him to "at least" add our signs—my mountains and Sarah's leaf—so we can tell who is who. Funny how much I want to be seen as myself, not just as a generic teacher-figure.

But then I consider the story Avery is actually illustrating: in this fictional world, Sarah and I are nothing but bystanders to action led by a courageous, powerful, and resourceful team of Children Firsters. We are no help at all—we're not even ON the playground when the action unfolds. I'm glad that I caught myself before insisting that Avery give us arms. In this story, teachers don't NEED arms!

Momentum, Flow, and Finishing

We finish up Chapter 2 just before Spring Break, and I get it written up to send to Pam later that week, just before the children return.

> It's the last day of spring break, and already most of my "school-mind" is turning toward our tradition of making Welcome Books to give the kids who are coming next fall... and then it's on toward Graduation. But hopefully, there will still be time and energy for bad guys...
>
> I'm curious where the kids will be when they come back tomorrow. I'm quite certain that those who have been working on the chapter book are going to want to do a third chapter, if for no other reason than that Alena, Elisabeth and Miles have not had their turn to illustrate yet. I plan to convene the group tomorrow for an initial conversation. I really have no idea what to bring other than, "What are you thinking about Chapter 3?" and I'm prepared for the conversation to be rocky, since the initial conversation about Chapter 2 was so rough...

Pam's response leaves me feeling confident and excited...

> I agree with your instinct to invite thinking about Chapter 3 with just a "Who has an idea for Chapter 3?" or some such. The children know the process now, and you may be surprised by where they decide to take the story (you also may not be surprised, but you CAN'T be surprised if you offer too much at this point). It will be interesting to see where the children's thinking will go. They have evolved this idea so much, developed so much clarity (even when they disagree), and their negotiating and representational skills have grown so much in these few months.

As it turns out, Pam is right. I ask my simple question—"What are you thinking about Chapter 3?"—and the children are off and running, reminding me periodically to "write this down." Their story, which builds and expands on the important themes in Chapter 2, emerges in one big rush of cooperative conversation, and becomes even more detailed and nuanced in the two follow-up conversations in which the children work out inconsistencies and add details.

They build this new story around a character drawn from real-life headlines: a robotic bad guy with the voice and face of Donald Trump.

The arrival of this character is, to say the least, an interesting moment. Since the election, we've heard very little from the children about the real-life President, but I know he figures quite prominently in the buzz of adult conversation all around them. None of the adults in our school community "like" Donald Trump, and most are

Parker sketched a generic robot—not a bad guy in and of itself—with the face of Donald Trump emblazoned on its chest.

genuinely alarmed by his actions and offended by his demeanor. But our general stance at school has been to set those worries aside each morning and focus on something we can feel good about: providing a safe and nurturing place for our children to grow up. After election day came and went, we heard little or nothing about Donald Trump from the children, and they have not heard anything about him from the Children First teachers, either. But in this moment, as the kids speak his name and bring their particular sense of his "badness" into their work, I trust that they are looking for a way to grapple on their own terms with the general miasma of worry and anger they associate with this looming figure.

And I appreciate that they are not declaring war on the real Donald Trump, human being and politician. Rather, they are stepping up to battle an evil robot to whom they have given his face and his voice. I think of the Donald Trump children see and hear on TV, on car radios, on newspaper pages: the seemingly omnipresent images and sound bites that they likely associate with anxious and disgusted responses from their grown-ups. And of course, children are exquisitely tuned social creatures, sensitive to body language and tone of voice, actively engaged in developing a code of social conduct based on what they have been taught by trusted grown-ups, and on what they have experienced directly in community with one another. The children know full-well that threatening, boasting, belittling, and name-calling are not friendly ways of navigating the world. Apart from what they have heard from their parents, the children seem to have their own sensory impression of how distasteful this character's behavior is. Enough with the vague worry about this Donald Trump guy, they seem to be saying: we are taking charge.

And here I am, witness and scribe. Certainly, I am in full agreement with the children's evaluation of this figure's behavior and demeanor, but they aren't looking for my agreement or approval. Moreover, I notice that I am studiously resisting any "fun" or personal satisfaction I might find in commiserating with them about President Donald Trump. This is their work, not mine, and I am not about to indulge myself at the expense of their autonomy and hard-won clarity. Nor does it occur to me to push back against the children's idea for the sake of avoiding controversy or "teaching respect" for government institutions. The last thing I'd want to do is to make an important and worrisome topic "unspeakable" or "taboo."

Of course, if one of the kids had piped up to say, "My Daddy voted for Donald Trump" or "I like Donald Trump" or "Oliver's family likes Donald Trump" then this would have been a very different conversation. As with any difference of opinion—and especially with a potentially tender disclosure around family identity—I would have slowed the process down and made space for each of the kids to name their truth, to ask each other questions in a spirit of curiosity, and to use their "active listening" skills.

Safeguarding a process for hearing and honoring each other's perspectives is a basic teacher responsibility. While I would not jump in to censor the children's thinking or direct their decision-making, I would MARCH in to make space for a heartfelt exchange of perspectives and life experiences. So, in a hypothetical conversation in which someone at the table expressed a soft spot for Donald Trump, I'm certain we would have come around to a question like, "Are you saying you're not OK with giving the bad guy Robot the face and voice of Donald Trump?" I would have worked to make sure there was room at the table for everyone, and that none of these authors would leave the writer's room feeling alienated or disconnected from the chapter book they were creating together.

And in that hypothetical situation, this chapter might well have featured a different version of bombastic bad guy.

But this day, at this table, for these children, Robot Donald Trump was not a casual choice, or a controversial choice. He was born in a moment when swirling worry and a sense of some brewing dis-ease and wrongness was brought to ground and integrated and handled, by the community of kids, together. I could feel them gathering their collective power to take care of a problem their adults were worrying about, but did not seem to be fixing. I can imagine a different day and a different conversation where the bad guy summoned up would be "Bad Guy Covid19" or "Pollution Man" or "Carbon Footprint" or "Racist Guy."

So, in the moment that Robot Donald Trump is born, I remain authentically neutral—unsurprised, and neither questioning nor affirming—as I scribe and reflect back the wave of narrative that follows.

Here's the final version of Chapter 3:

Chapter 3: Robot

After the Children Firsters saved them from the playground monster, the visitor boy and his parents say, "Bye! We're going on a train to Antarctica because we don't want to get hit by any more bad guys."

But the Children Firsters say, "Well, you might see a bad guy in Antarctica, because we once went there and we had a battle with Robot Donald Trump, but he did not die in that battle." And the visitors say, "OK, we want to watch you fight him again." And the Children Firsters say, "OK, call our clock when you see him."

Alena draws the visiting boy and his parents leaving Children First for Antarctica, because they want to get away from bad guys.

When the visitors get to Antarctica, they call Cell Phone 911, and the Children Firsters hear all the alarms—it's so loud because all of them went off—and they see that the hand on their clock is pointing to Robot Donald Trump.

Each Children Firster has one part of a bad-guy fighting robot hidden in their own closets. And the robot is connected to the clock, so when the alarm goes off and it's pointing to Robot Donald Trump, the Children Firsters bring their parts out into the hallway and meet up in a place that is right in the middle of the 12 houses.

When they get there and the pieces are close together, the kids just let go of their parts and then robot attaches itself together. Their Robot is as big as a skyscraper in New York, and it has bones on the outside.

Miles draws a bad guy alarm clock pointing to Robot Donald Trump.

Elisabeth shows the Children First robot after it "attaches itself together."

The kids climb through the bottom of the robot, from youngest to oldest, and each of them controls a different part of the robot. They use the ladder to get to their part of the robot. Oliver stands on the bottom with Aiden, and they control the feet.

Then come Mical and Maya in the lower belly. Avery and Alena are near the arms; Avery controls the right arm, and Alena controls the left. And then Elisabeth and Lia at the upper belly. And then Finn at the neck, and Sam by the nose and mouth. Then Parker and Miles on top, controlling the eyes and ears.

Each part of the robot can transform into a tiny invisible jet, one for each Children Firster. So they transform their Robot into twelve tiny jets, and the jets take off with fire coming out, and then they turn invisible. The Children Firsters fly their invisible jets all at the same speed, so they are right next to each other in the sky, twelve in a row.

Alena maps the battle stations of the Children Firsters (represented by their signs) inside their robot.

Miles draws one of the twelve "tiny and invisible" jets—labeled with a spiral to indicate that it is part of the Children First team—on its way to Antarctica.

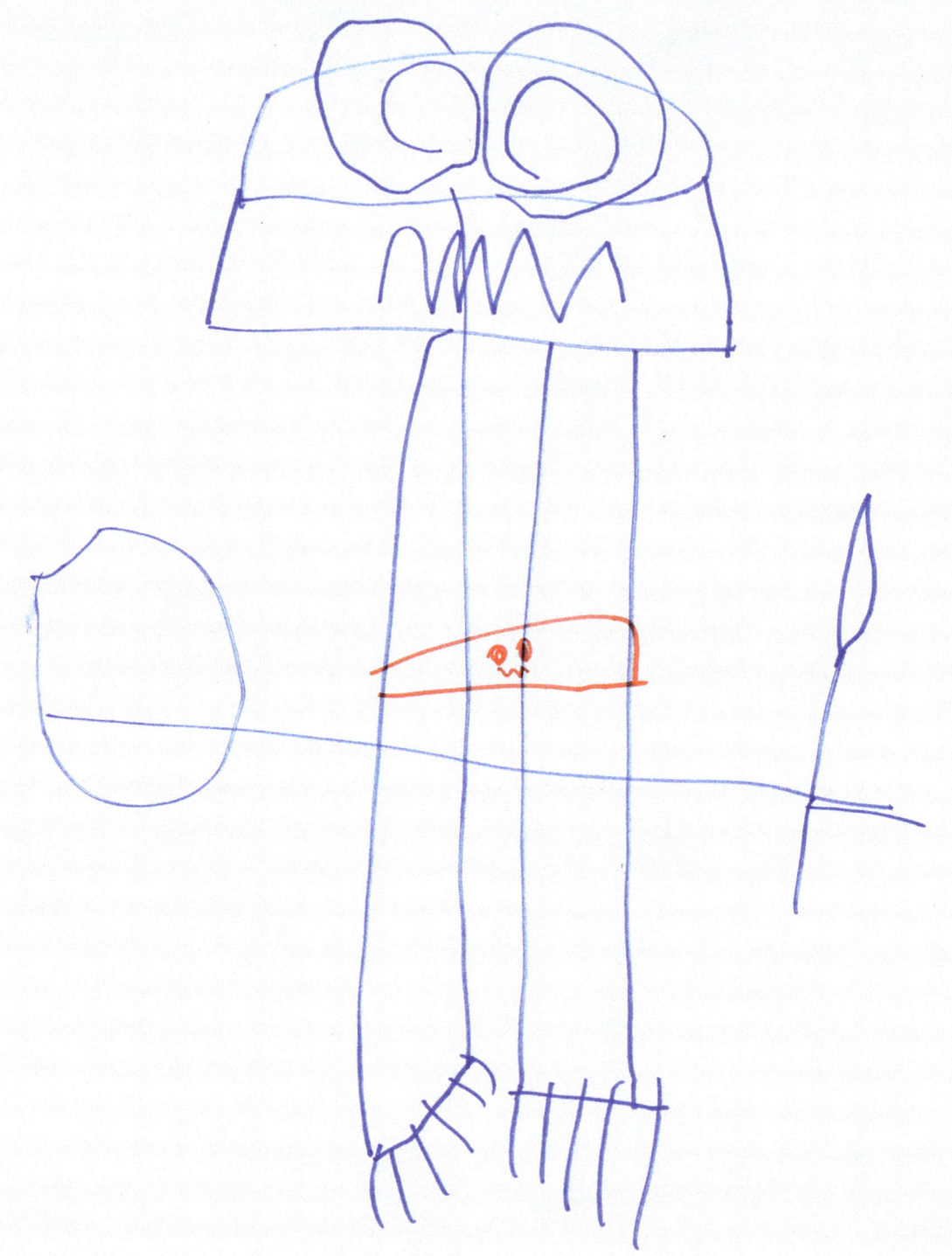

When they get to Antarctica, Robot Donald Trump is standing at the greeting of the airport. He is as big as a regular Donald Trump with a picture of Donald Trump's face on his chest where his voice comes out, and he has a shooter and sword and shield he uses to hurt people.

The Children Firsters transform their invisible jets back into the Robot, and now the Robot is invisible, too. Robot Donald Trump does not know they are there and can't figure out who is about to fight him, but the Children Firsters wear their goggles inside the robot, so they can always see each other.

Then they battle the Robot Donald Trump. All the different Children Firsters have swords and shooters and shields, and they all stand near little holes in the robot so they can shoot stuff out at him. If a Children Firster is close to Robot Donald Trump, the other Children Firsters give them their shooters and swords and shields to use, too.

Parker and Miles control the eyes and the ears. They have the important job of looking to see where Robot Donald Trump is going, so the Children Firsters know where to shoot.

Sam controls the mouth. He says, "I don't like you!"

OPPOSITE PAGE: Elisabeth shows Robot Donald Trump at the "greeting of the airport." **ABOVE LEFT:** Elisabeth shows two Children Firsters wearing their goggles inside the Children First robot. **ABOVE RIGHT:** Miles draws Sam, who controls the Children First robot's mouth and shouts, "I don't like you!"

PURSUING BAD GUYS

Finn shoots from the neck of the Robot. Lia and Elisabeth are shooting from the middle of the Robot. Maya and Mical are shooting from the belly down near the legs.

Avery and Alena push the button to turn on the arms and then they punch Robot Donald Trump right in the eye and he can't see anything. Then they punch him in the belly. He says "Ow! Ow!"

Oliver and Aiden are at the bottom, and they push the button to turn on the feet, then turn the knob to lift the feet up and—STOMP!

STOMP!—they smash the Robot Donald Trump as flat as a splat-ball and he dies. Then Oliver controls the right leg to kick the splat-ball Robot Donald Trump into the water. They all cheer, "Whoo hoo! He's disgusting!"

When the Robot Donald Trump is dead in the water, the Children Firsters transform their Robot back into jets, and fly back home to Durham. They each go to their houses, and lay down with their clocks next to them. They put in earplugs, since their clock alarms are so loud, and then they go to sleep. The end.

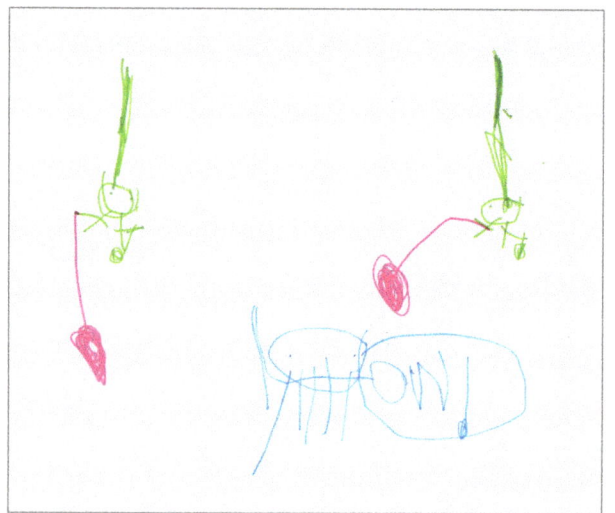 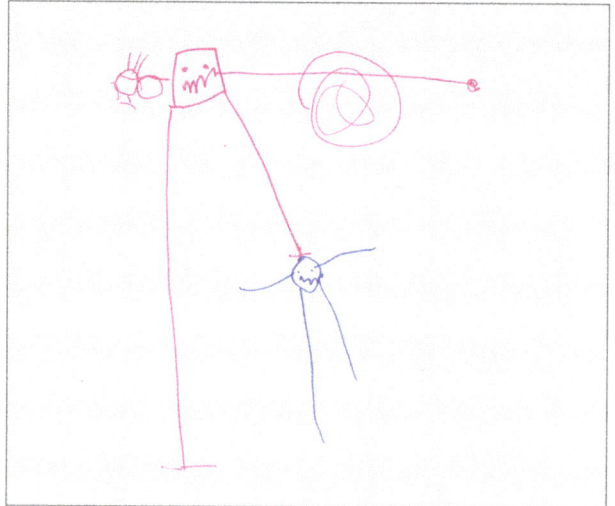

ABOVE LEFT: Alena draws herself and Avery as they control the robot's arms, and make it punch Robot Donald Trump, who yells, "Ow!" **ABOVE RIGHT:** Miles shows the Children First robot stomping—with satisfying finality—on Robot Donald Trump. **OPPOSITE PAGE:** Miles shows what happens when the Children First robot "transforms" into the 12 children's individual jets—each identified by its sign—all headed home to their own houses for some well-deserved rest.

The Good Guys Take the Day

Reflecting on Chapter 3, I am awestruck by the children's declaration of personal and collective courage. I think back to the despair and fear in our community after the election in November, and all the worried and angry conversations kids have been hearing among their grown-ups ever since. For the kids, the specter of Donald Trump is everywhere, a shadowy figure of horror and ridicule hanging over dinner table and playground conversations.

So, there's nothing random about Avery's idea that the Bad Guy is a robot version of Donald Trump, or Parker's declaration that the Children Firsters had "battled him once before and lost." It occurs to me that, in this chapter, the children accomplish what their adults had failed to do: they get rid of that Bad Guy. And notice that, in this chapter, they do not wait for the Bad Guy to invade their space; they go on an epic journey—all the way to Antarctica—to find him and face him down. They pursue the Badness, and then bring all their tricks to bear on the battle that follows.

Pam connects this aspect of the story with all the trickiness the kids are bringing to their pretend play: Wow, the bad guy stuff has evolved! It is my experience that tricking danger only happens when children have developed a certain confidence in themselves through this kind of play... Their play and their narrative are on the same page and it seems they got there together, as a group. That's evolutionary, as well. The clock part of the story seems almost summative. Sam says, "When it's on the smiley faces it means the bad guys aren't there. And when it's on the bad guy it means the bad guys are there," and he includes every KIND of bad guy. Like saying "Here are all the kinds of danger we are tricking." The children have become so powerful!

I think about the unapologetic violence in this story, and in the first two chapters, and reflect on why I don't feel squeamish about it. The children are clearly hearkening back to the original premise of their Bad Guy play and stories: When something is really, really, REALLY bad, you've got to stop it and stop it for real and forever. The fictional villains they create for these chapters are thoroughly irredeemable, not characters who behave badly, but characters who embody badness itself.

The stories are allegory. It's Good versus Evil, and the children are Good. With our tricks and our team, they are saying—on behalf of ourselves and those weaker than ourselves, without grown-ups to help, to the point of exhaustion, without giving up—we will put a stop to this Badness.

As Chapter 3 opens, the children shoulder the responsibility to safeguard the vulnerable "little kid" whose life they already saved in Chapter 2. As Chapter 3 ends, Mission Accomplished, our heroes crawl under the covers and put in their earplugs, but even then their alarm clocks are primed to send the next alert.

> The children are acknowledging that the work of the courageous is never done.

They seem to be saying "This big work is tiring, and those loud clocks really jangle the nerves, but doing good is also necessary and exhilarating, and—as long as I have some snacks and a plane that takes me back home to sleep—I will have the resources I need to meet the challenge."

And of course, the primary resource that fuels this courage is Community. In Chapter 2, our heroes are part of a team that defeats Badness with the simple power of greater numbers. But in Chapter 3, they take the idea of Team much further and deeper: here, they work as a team in one literal body, in which every child has a specific and essential role, organized carefully from oldest at the head, to youngest at the feet.

And back in "real life" we are seeing the same courage and resolve. We see it in the "wrassling" on the playground; in the climbing and adventuring at the Eno River; and especially in the vulnerability and presence the children are bringing to social and emotional challenges. These are brave children who are braver together. Wise pedagogical leader that she is, Pam reminds us often to ask ourselves, "How are the children changing?" As we begin to prepare our reflections for end-of-year conferences, we are convinced that each child has moved into a more confident, connected and empowered place.

And that's true for me, too. Making the chapter book held powerful learning about my role as co-constructor of an in-depth project. I saw how I make and operate from assumptions, and how those assumptions can close down the creative process of co-construction. I got better at noticing all the ways I go too fast, miss important moments, and offer either/or questions instead of open-ended invitations to think.

> But most of all, I began finding the courage to be an openly—even joyfully—imperfect teacher, to be a grown-up who is a bit more like a child: curious, alive, and unashamedly becoming.

I share this self-reflection with Pam, who responds with just the insight and encouragement I need from my pedagogical companion:

> Donna, you are asking yourself the questions that need to be asked. Becoming more conscious, I think, of the power of your stance in dialogue with children. By recognizing when you may have stepped too far or gone too fast, you are setting yourself up for making different decisions the next time. It's really the only way this learning can happen, and in my opinion, you've boarded the train. Not that you will never regret an interaction…you probably always will, at times. But with practice, you learn how certain expressions support or hinder children's process, and the regretful moments become fewer and farther between.

CHAPTER 8

GOODBYE TO THE FADING BAD GUY

We've been at the Bad Guy research all winter and spring; suddenly, it's May, and our days are filled with talk and plans of Graduation, now only a month away. Alena and Aiden are filling the bird feeder at the library, where they pause to study the fading Library Bad Guy. We know him so well by now! In addition to writing stories about him, we've spent time making maps and models to represent our theories about where he lives. The kids have interacted with him often in their pretend play, and even make a point of introducing him to visitors. So, of course they notice when he begins to change...

Alena:	I think some of the markers go away.
Donna:	I can still see his face.
Alena:	But not the other parts. I think the markers were not a good idea.
Donna:	Do you feel sad he's disappearing, or do you think it's good he's going away? I mean, he is a bad guy.

Alena: I'm sad.
Aiden: Sad.
Alena: If it was a real bad guy, I was going to be happy.

A couple of weeks later, I stop a small group of kids who are playing near the library to ask what they make of these changes…

Parker: The sun is making it fade.
Lia: And the rain is washing it away.
Donna: What do you feel about the bad guy fading and washing away?
Miles: Good, because he's gonna turn good.
Parker: Yeah, right.

Crafting Rituals around Goodbyes

By now, we are deep into the season of remembering, gratitude and goodbyes, a time of many carefully crafted rituals. Each child graduating from Children First has already had a "Special Day" including an intimate and often teary gathering in the Library we call a "progress conference," where the graduator sits with parents and teachers to share delicious food and hear stories of learning and growth, stories that we represent with beads that the child then uses to make a beautiful "Graduation Necklace." Graduation itself—the big party where the whole community will gather to honor the graduators—is only five school days away. It's time for us to decide how we'll say goodbye to what's left of the Library Bad Guy.

I bring the question to the older kids at lunch, in a conversation which goes everywhere yet nowhere conclusive. Maybe we should take the Library Bad Guy down right away and just recycle him. Or cut him into pieces and take the pieces home. Maybe he should be at graduation, but maybe graduation is NOT a place for bad guys at all. Maybe he should have his own goodbye meeting. Plenty of cheerful thinking, but no consensus.

When Sarah and I talk later about the options the children have suggested, we realize that we have our own strong ideas about a fitting goodbye ceremony for this character who has been such an important part of our lives this year.

> In general, we believe that teachers have an important responsibility for shaping classroom culture, and that includes crafting rituals around goodbyes of all kinds.

We have structures in place to support the everyday goodbyes that go along with arriving at school and leaving for home. When a beloved handyman or substitute teacher or student helper moves on, we mark the event with songs and handmade gifts and goodbye hugs. And graduation season is a whole month of activity that foregrounds the momentous goodbye between our school and the children who are graduating. We always give time and attention to important endings.

So what about a goodbye for the Library Bad Guy? Sarah and I agree that this ending is important, too. It's important to *us*; we feel great affection for this character and what he represents about this adventure we've been on together with the children. And because we've been watching so closely, we know that the Library Bad Guy is important to the kids as well.

We wonder about structuring this goodbye in the familiar shape of a funeral. We are a school that advocates what we call "death practice"—looking at death squarely, with curiosity and openness, as a defining fact of life and a profound commonality among every living thing. We draw and discuss dead animals that we encounter; we study natural objects in various stages of decay; we sing songs and read books and invite lots of open conversation about death. Funerals have been an important part of our life together at school this year, as they are every year. We have a simple but very particular ritual for marking the deaths of pets, and for honoring wild animals whose bodies we find at the creek or playground. We've talked extensively about the funeral of Martin Luther King, and children have shared their own experiences with funerals. My dear friend Maureen, a founding Children First parent, died suddenly just a month ago, and the children have heard a lot about her life and death this spring. So, we know that the kids will not be surprised by this suggestion.

I come to my next lunch with the old-timers prepared to share our proposal, but also determined to stay open and responsive to the children's responses.

Donna: I have a conversation here from awhile ago. I want to read you this part. I asked, "What do you feel about the bad guy fading away?" and Miles said, "Good, because he's going to turn good." And Parker said, "Yeah." That made me wonder: Is the Library Bad Guy still bad, or is he good now?

Miles: Good.
Parker: A silly bad guy. Ever since we made it we thought he was silly. Now he's even sillier.
Donna: Sarah and I actually think it would be a good idea to find a way to say goodbye to the Library Bad Guy when we're all together at school. So we were trying to think about it. One idea was to cut him up and recycle him. But then I was thinking: when we take the Library Bad Guy down, is it kind of like he dies? Is it the end of his life?
Many: Yeah.
Donna: So, yeah. I was wondering if he needs a funeral.

As we expected, the kids take this idea up immediately and with enthusiasm.

Parker: Paper funerals, with papers hanging up with pictures of bad guys and all.
Donna: I know two different ways that people do funerals to say goodbye to bodies. One is that they bury them.
Many: Yeah.
Donna: And the other is that they burn them.
Parker: Piece of paper, burn the piece of paper.
Elisabeth: It's really a drawing on a piece of paper.
Donna: And we've buried things in the garden.
Alena: Birds.
Parker: And fish. Remember Coconut and Pumpkin?

after sharing some memories of those lovely little fish...

Parker: How would you burn it?
Donna: I think we would just make a fire in the fire pit.

Fire is an important and familiar part of life at Children First. All winter, kids have worked with Sarah on building and cooking over fires in our portable playground fire pit.

Donna: Do you think we should sing something?
Miles: Jesus, Jesus.

Miles is singing the name of "Jesus" to the tune of a simple but deeply reverent Mr. Rogers song called "Tree Tree Tree," a song we adapt in many ways at school, including for funerals, where we sing the name of the dead creature we are burying. Although Miles is not a practicing Christian, I think he invokes the name of "Jesus" to affirm the sacredness of the ritual.

Parker: No - "Bad Guy, Bad Guy, Bad Guy."

Parker is singing, to demonstrate how we could put the Bad Guy's name into the song, the way we normally would in a funeral.

Donna: Oh, like we always sing at funerals... And should we go around and say one thing we remember about the Library Bad Guy, like we usually do at funerals?
Many: Yeah.
Donna: I'm glad we're going to say a serious goodbye to our Library Bad Guy. It feels important.

When I say, "It feels important" I'm purposefully bringing a sense of gravitas to this moment, inviting the kids to take our work together seriously, and to treat their collective experience with reverence. If they had responded to our funeral idea with mirth or disinterest, I would have backed off. But I can tell that this plan feels as right to them as it does to me and Sarah. Together, we put a date for the funeral on the Kid Calendar.

The Funeral

As kids arrive on the morning of the funeral, many of them follow Parker's lead and draw quick images of bad guys to "decorate" for the funeral.

Once everyone arrives, we gather in our meeting circle on the bike deck, with the fire pit in the center.

As Sarah carefully pulls the Library Bad Guy down from the place he has occupied on the library wall since January, we sing several rounds of "Bad Guy, Bad Guy, Bad Guy" to the tune of "Tree Tree Tree." The kids' mood is happy and humorous, but also respectful and thoughtful. I think their ability to modulate their energy and rest into this "ritual space" is quite remarkable. They seem to "read" the sense of occasion Sarah and I create with our own reverent energy as we experience the weight and sweetness of this ending.

Sarah slowly makes her way to the circle, carrying the Library Bad Guy in her arms. We stop singing and take a moment to share "something you remember or like about the bad guy." A few highlights from our trip around the circle, in which each child spoke in turn:

Oliver:	I liked about him when he was still here.
Aiden:	I liked when he was staying on the library.
Elisabeth:	I liked when he had a whole body and when he was just made and we were running away from him.
Avery:	I liked when he protect the whole school.

Sarah and I share our own memories, and then I invite the group to take a deep breath together, and say "Thank you, Bad Guy!"

Sarah begins quietly tearing the Library Bad Guy into pieces, moving with deliberation and care. She counts quietly, and some of the kids count with her.

Once she has 12 pieces, she calls Oliver, the youngest child, gives him a piece and shows him how to crumple it up. He crumples his part and adds it to the fire pit, then sits back down. From Oliver all the way around to Miles, the kids take turns in an unhurried and serious way to do their part. The children, fully absorbed, lean in to watch.

Once all 12 parts are resting in the firepit, Sarah lights the paper. We watch, spellbound, as the pieces burst into flames and then begin to change—crinkling, darkening, and disappearing into the fire. The spectacle is visually arresting, and there is much exclaiming as the changes unfold.

Then something truly amazing happens. The wind picks up and begins blowing the ashes of the Library Bad Guy, first in a snowy swirl back toward the library, then all around our circle. Many kids have ashes near their feet or in their hair. It is as though our Bad Guy is saying his own farewell to his old home on the library wall, then dispersing himself all around the playground and over the group. We are stunned, then delighted. All around the circle, there are cries of "What?! He's on me!" and "Wow! He's on you!" and "Look what's happening!"

When the ashes are almost gone, we stand together and I invite us to take one big breath in, then let it out. As we release the breath, we instinctively lean closer to blow the remaining ashes. Then we take a few last deep breaths and say our final "goodbye." The circle of children disperses with laughter; Sarah and I share a hug; and fifteen minutes later, we are rehearsing for Graduation.

CHAPTER 9

REFLECTING ON LEARNING AND CHANGE

The Bad Guy funeral is a particularly magical moment, but we have seen many others like it this spring. We have learned that tapping into the power of core Children First curriculum—storytelling, portraiture, pretend play, mapping, surveys, making, or, in this case, death practice—can yield riches for our Bad Guy Research.

Once again, I see that this long-term investigation is not happening INSTEAD of our usual curriculum, but is happening INSIDE it.

The teachers and children built this investigation together, but it rose from the strong foundation teachers had already cemented in place: a rich and responsive learning environment; support for fluency in many expressive languages; and most of all, loving and respectful relationship between and among the children and their adults. That foundation grounded us in belonging and purpose; it provided the sense of security that allowed us all to wonder, create and grow.

So what's different, now, because of our year with Pam and the bad guys? Looking back, I am struck by a central paradox in Pam's guidance. On the one hand, she told us, approach the Bad Guy Research with no particular end in mind. Our charge was to follow the children's energy and trust that any work genuinely aligned with their intentions would have meaning and positive impact. At the same time, she urged us to watch for evidence of that impact and meaning. Maybe we were not pursuing specific outcomes, but as teacher-researchers, we were certainly paying attention to what came from the children's examination of bad guys.

> According to Pam, shaping a retrospective narrative about learning and change—telling our own story of the children's story—would be an important exercise for our own learning.

Some of this reflection and analysis happened immediately and naturally, as we mined our bad guy documentation for evidence of ways that individual children had grown and changed through the winter and spring. In our end of year conferences with parents, stories of courage and teamwork took center stage.

But we had yet to reflect deeply on the story of the 13th Child: the whole group and its teachers. And then summer came with its own urgencies and distractions, and, despite my best intentions, a new school year arrived and I had yet to pick up all the pieces of the Bad Guy Research and put them back together into one coherent story. It was the invitation from Ann and Margie to write this book that finally called me back to Pam's provocation to step back and look at the big picture.

And what do I see?

We have stunning individual growth. There is Finn claiming responsibility for protecting the playground he shares with kids who have slowly

but surely become his friends, and young Oliver finding his sense of belonging in the very middle of the bad guy pretending. There is Mical using her stories to find a moral compass, and Miles' proud effort to capture the full regalia of the Children First air force flying home from Antarctica in his careful drawing. There is Alena's assertive insistence on coming to the big kid table, and Lia's determination and vulnerability in bringing us, again and again, to the critical questions of whether bad guys are real and whether children are safe. There is Elisabeth's newfound courage in the face of suspense, and Avery's resolve to speak his truth when he offers his older friends the brilliant insight that leads us out of confusion and straight to the power of archetype in our Chapter Book. There is Sam establishing his moral authority, insisting on inclusion, and Parker finding the flexibility and trust to believe that inclusion does not have to end in disappointing compromise. For each and every individual Bad Guy Researcher, there is a story of learning and change.

We have some beautiful artifacts—namely the Clay Protectors and the Chapter Book: creations that manifest the children's intent and ability and vision, and that become gifts to the community, traces of these children and their

work that will last far beyond the time we were together physically.

And for me and Sarah?

As I write these concluding paragraphs, another full year has come and gone. When we returned to school in the Fall of 2017, the Bad Guys were with us still, but they did not claim center stage. In fact, we had a year of Children First much like the 27 years that came before the Bad Guy year, a rich and meaningful year, but one without any singular preoccupation or compelling subject for research. I admit to some dejected moments, times when I found myself thinking, "Maybe the Bad Guy Research was a fluke, and nothing like that will ever happen here again."

Maybe not. But Sarah and I are still learning and experimenting. This year, we committed ourselves to regular practices that bolster the capacity of the 13th child: more conversation with the whole group at meeting; more small group conversation around daily drawing practice; and a regular habit of bringing documentation back to the group for further consideration. And perhaps most important, we adopted Pam's protocol for looking at documentation together as teachers, and we try to make time for those conversations every single week. We are learning to move from observation to action, and we are doing it together.

And internally, for me?

I have long believed that, if I truly love something, I must be willing to let that thing take hold of my heart and change me.

I loved the Bad Guy Research, and it did change me. As I was considering what to say here about my own learning, I happened to pick up a book that had been on my "to read" list for several years: *Mindset*, by Carol Dweck. Anyone familiar with Dweck's wildly popular research has probably already diagnosed my chronic issues with "fixed mindset thinking:" the aversion to risk, the need to be right, the skepticism about my capacity to learn new things. But I think my year with Bad Guys loosened the binds of that confining way of being in the world, and allowed me to creep a little further toward the "growth mindset" end of the spectrum.

My thinking is a bit more open, my curiosity more awake. These days, I may be more afraid of stagnation than I am of mistakes!

I put that emerging growth mindset to work this year as we invited children to explore some juicy ideas, sparked by our genuine curiosity about themes we saw in their play, stories and visual work: "What's danger?" "How do people grow their courage?" "Where do dreams come from?"

"Can we teachers step into the current of learning and becoming WITH the children?" That was the question that led us to Pam, our intrepid pedagogical companion. After a year of riding that current with Pam and the bad guys, we have our answer: "We certainly can!" What we've still to discover are the hundred interesting directions and beautiful destinations where the current may carry us next.

ACKNOWLEDGEMENTS

The story I tell in these pages is an exercise in meaning making and truth telling, and not the "final report" of an analyst back from a fact-finding mission. I'm speaking my truth about the meaning I was making and have made about a particular year in my teaching life. It's both humbling and reassuring to know that Parker, Sam and Miles; Elisabeth, Lia and Alena; Avery, Aiden and Finn; Maya, Mical and Oliver—each child who figures in this narrative—not to mention the many adults who are part of the story—my co-teacher Sarah, our pedagogical companion, Pam, and every Children First parent—any and all would likely tell this story a different way. I'm not trying to tell THE story FOR anyone; I've just tried to tell ONE version of the story the truest way I can. I so hope it lands well for everyone who was there. And I am grateful, beyond any words I can muster, to every one of those real life "characters" who lived and learned inside this story with me.

ABOUT THE AUTHOR

In 1990, Donna King took what she learned from her graduate school research on child care quality, and partnered with a group of teachers and parents to launch a small, non-profit early education program in Durham, North Carolina.

They named the school "Children First" to affirm their founding commitment: in this place, parents and teachers would come together to grapple with the harsh economic realities of early childhood education—high cost for families, low compensation for teachers—without compromising the experience of the children in their care.

Children First currently serves 12 children, aged 2 ¾ to 5, in one mixed-age group with two teachers. Over its thirty-year history, the school has taken to heart the core ideals of progressive education: intention, reflection, joy, beauty, respect, lifelong learning, and love. It strives to foster a close-knit and lively community where children are seen and celebrated as unique individuals; where children spend lots of time outdoors and grow a deep connection with nature; where children learn to communicate their feelings and thoughts through many expressive languages, especially the native language of childhood—pretend play; and where children's unfolding life stories are captured in individual portfolios that document their development as creators, thinkers, citizens and friends.

Donna is married to Kevin McClain, whose quiet wisdom and unstinting generosity are the hidden backbone of Children First, and the beating heart of the King-McClain family. Their three children—Cara, Anna Grace, and Josh—all Children First graduates—are now young adults, each working in their own unique ways to bring the values of Children First to life in the larger world.

Avery's drawing of Donna and Sarah for the Welcome Book for new children—including their signs, the mountains and the leaf.

STUDY GUIDE

From Reading to Thinking: A Protocol for Reflection and Learning

Pursuing Bad Guys holds stories within stories, one unfolding into another. There's the story of children's pretend play about good guys and bad guys, and of their story-telling about confrontations with villains. There's the story of Donna's journey into a new role as an educator, and the story of the pedagogical companion who walked that journey with her. In all these stories, we read reflections on the practice of studying children's work in order to gain a better understanding of their pursuits. We read descriptions of the ways in which children use representational languages like drawing and sculpting to give eloquent voice to their questions and insights. We read about the rhythms of teacher research and of collaborative inquiry among children, educators, and families. This book is an intricate narrative and deserves substantial study.

Consider reading *Pursuing Bad Guys* several times, choosing one of the many stories to particularly follow. You might set yourself a few study questions as you read:

- What can I learn about the necessary role of trustworthy companions on a quest?

- What can I learn about the power of storytelling? The power of listening to and studying stories?

- What can I learn about the ways in which representational languages invite new possibilities for thinking and collaborating?

- What can I learn from Donna and from the children about the learning that happens at the intersection of emotional and intellectual risk-taking?

Another way to approach this book is to consider the role of disequilibrium in sparking growth. Donna writes, "Starting is awkward: you feel you have to give up things that are dear to you, and that's painful, and you're not sure it's going to work out. You could just let kids play, and provision well for that: it'll never be wrong, it's familiar and safe and easy. But you could step towards a whole new place: your longing for that becomes stronger than staying with what you know, and so you take the step." We hear her wrestle with complex internal dynamics, which you may find resonate with your own teaching practice:

- Feeling inspired to change while continuing to cherish traditions;

- Wanting the support of a pedagogical companion but appreciating your autonomy and feeling hesitant about being vulnerable, afraid of having your mistakes witnessed;

- Balancing a classroom culture between a focus on individual children and a focus on shaping a collective identity as a group;

- Claiming a role for yourself in children's pursuits without imposing an agenda that derails children's play;

- Honoring children's right to ferocious bad guy play and nurturing values for non-violence, kindness, and respect for differences.

You may see other dynamic tugs to add to this list, either in Donna's story or in your own evolution as an educator. Notice which of these sparks some especially strong response in you—unease and uncertainty, or the feeling of closely-held values being challenged, or a longing to understand how you might better navigate that dynamic in your own practice. Make time to do some writing to uncover what's inside that response for you.

After this initial exploration, move into more thinking and study using a protocol to guide you. Here are some questions for you to consider, built on the guideposts in the Thinking Lens protocol (as described in *From Teaching to Thinking: A Pedagogy for Reimagining Our Work*). We offer these to support your study and to help you articulate your learning, perhaps in writing, and then in conversation with colleagues and pedagogical companions.

Know yourself. Open your heart to this moment.
What touched you about this story?

How were your values reflected in or challenged by the values that Donna and Sarah use to guide their practice?

In this book, the children do a lot of loud, tough, and fierce pretend play and storytelling. How did that land for you?

Donna writes about letting her longing start her on a journey into a new way of teaching. Do you hear longings calling to you? What gets in the way of acting on those longings? What might help you begin to change in the ways you long to change?

Take the children's points of view.
Why do you think children are so compelled by both *being* and *banishing* badness?

How do you see the children in this book express their desire to expand their courage and competency?

In what ways do you see the children express something parallel to your own feelings and thoughts about bad guys in the world and how they should be handled?

Examine the environment.
What was already in place in the social-emotional environment at Children First that allowed this investigation to take off?

What aspects of the culture and routines of Children First intrigue you with possibilities for your own work?

How does the use of the outdoor environment at Children First provoke you to reconsider possibilities for your program?

Collaborate with others to expand perspectives.
As you discuss this story with others, listen for conflicting perspectives. Do your colleagues think about key ideas in this book differently than you do? Take up those differences together, rather than slip past them.

What learning theories are you curious about, after reading this story? Consider arenas such as the co-construction of knowledge; art media as thinking tools; vulnerability and risk-taking as cornerstones for learning. How will you find out more about what intrigues or challenges or stymies you?

What do you understand about the value of a pedagogical companion? How might you find such a colleague?

Reflect and take action.
Building on your reflections, write a statement that describes the learning that you will carry with you from *Pursuing Bad Guys*.

What will you do differently in your work, because of reading this book?

Reading a book is an investment of time and attention. To make the most of that investment, revisit sections of the book that engaged or confused you. Find study companions to help you reflect on the story of *Pursuing Bad Guys*. Commit yourself to transform your reading from a passive experience of listening to a good story to an active engagement with thinking and questioning. Reading a book in this way becomes professional development.

As you carry *Pursuing Bad Guys* into your teaching practice, may you find energizing opportunities to transform your work in ways that honor your longings and hopes. And may you be lifted and supported by trustworthy companions who walk with you on your quest for courage and community.

—Ann Pelo and Margie Carter
    Editors of the *Reimagining Our Work* (ROW) Collection
    Authors of *From Teaching to Thinking: A Pedagogy for Reimagining Our Work*

www.ingramcontent.com/pod-product-compliance
Lightning Source LLC
Chambersburg PA
CBHW060922170426
43191CB00025B/2454